ALLERGY- FREE COOKING

How to Survive the Elimination Diet and Eat Happily Ever After

EILEEN RHUDE YODER, PH.D.

D0067204

Da Capo

LIFE
LONG

A Member of the Perseus Books Group

Portions of Chapter 5 are adapted from "Maintaining Patient Compliance During an Elimination Diet," from *Handbook of Food Allergy*, edited by James C. Breneman, Vol. 29, pp. 239–246 of the Immunology Series, © 1987 by Marcel-Dekker, Inc., New York, and reprinted with their kind permission.

Many of the designations used by manufacturers and sellers to distinguish their products are claimed as trademarks. Where these designations appear in the book and the author was aware of a trademark claim, the designations have been printed with initial capital letters—for example, Equal.

Library of Congress Cataloging-in-Publication Data
Yoder, Eileen Rhude.
    Allergy-free cooking.
    Bibliography; p.
    Includes index.
    1. Food allergy—Diet therapy—Recipes.
  I. Title.   .
RC588.D53Y63   1987   641.5'631   86-32136
ISBN 0-201-09797-4

Copyright © 1987 by Eileen Rhude Yoder, Ph.D.

All rights reserved. No part of this publication may be reproduced, stored in a retrieval system, or transmitted, in any form or by any means, electronic, mechanical, photocopying, recording, or otherwise, without the prior written permission of the publisher. Printed in the United States of America.

Cover design by Dorothea Sierra
Text design by Anna Post
Set in 11.5 point Cheltenham by DEKR Corp., Woburn, MA

To my parents, Diana and Howard Rhude,
and to my children, Laura and Patty,
with all my affection and appreciation.

CONTENTS

CONTENTS

FOREWORD

I have spent the past thirty years of my professional life treating people with food allergies. The technical and scientific elements of diagnosis and treatment have advanced amazingly in the last decade. However, the down-to-earth question of how and what to feed these patients has always been a problem. It has become even more difficult with the tremendous additions to our food supply. Instead of forty to fifty simple foods, our dietary intake now includes a possible 7,000 different foodstuffs, additives, chemicals, and drugs. Little wonder that the allergy diet poses a big problem for the preparer.

This book sets out to simplify and clarify. Dr. Yoder has spent many years studying the faults of available foods—and diets, looking for suppliers of pure foods and ingredients, and experimenting with food preparation. She shows clearly that one is able to provide a tasty, nutritious, yet safe diet for the allergic patient.

This product of Dr. Yoder's many years of study and work is a marvelous addition to the physician's tools. The difficult part—providing a diet for diagnosis and for treatment—can be handled expeditiously with this book. If a patient (or parent) can read, he or she should be able to maintain allergy-free nutrition without sacrificing the joy of eating. In fact, Dr. Yoder describes meal preparation in such detail that it sounds as though even I, a kitchen klutz, could do it— and have fun.

Allergy-Free Cooking is easy to use because it is well organized. The completeness of the presentation is represented by the twenty-seven recipes in the chapter on cookies, each sounding very original and delicious. Dr. Yoder has even found intriguing uses for bananas and nuts. Each recipe is presented in great detail and indicates whether the food is free of milk, eggs, wheat, corn, and other allergens, and whether it is suitable for the elimination diet.

Dr. Yoder has also given very practical methods for coping with traveling, holidays, and parties, all of which can be trying for the allergic patient. Various chapters describe shopping, substitutions, and precautions. Parents will find these eye-opening ideas a godsend.

I have always maintained that the allergic patient does not have to starve to death or be bored to death on an allergy diet. This book is readable proof of my conviction. I plan to use it extensively.

Allergy-Free Cooking comes at a most opportune time. Estimates suggest that over half of the U.S. population has ingestant problems, many allergic. This book will provide essential information to a great number of patients who probably have been waiting for such a practical book.

J. C. Breneman, M.D., A.B.A.I.
Four-time Chairman
International Food Allergy Symposium

PREFACE

My daughters, Laura and Patty, who are now teenagers, were sick from the day they were born. I took them from doctor to doctor. Finally, they were diagnosed as having severe allergies. And I also discovered I had just as many food allergies as they had!

It was a long time before we finally regained our health. The girls were sick much of the time and needed close medical supervision. However, we all learned to adjust our diets and not let food allergies limit our lifestyles. In fact, because of their allergies, I have encouraged the girls to be as active as possible. They are both adventurers; Laura has been camping and horseback riding in the Rocky Mountains, white-water rafting and mountain climbing in Idaho, jet skiing and wind surfing in Florida, and hang gliding in Tennessee! Patty is just as active, camping and traveling around the country, water and snow skiing, and participating on her school track and softball teams.

At first, however, it wasn't easy to adjust to having food allergies. I was discouraged with the bland and boring meals we were eating. I read every cookbook on food allergies available, but all I found were recipes that eliminated a few allergens such as milk, eggs, and wheat. At the time there weren't many books for people sensitive to other foods. So I went to different health food stores and bought interesting and unusual foods to add some flavor to our diets. I began to experiment with different ingredients and create new recipes. The results were terrific. I realized that despite our food allergies, we could still have delicious and exciting meals.

Along with my appetite for experimenting in the kitchen, I hungered for more information to help us understand and cope with our food

PREFACE

allergies. Being a nurse at the time, I went to the medical libraries and read everything I could on allergies. Slowly but surely I was gratified to see the study of food allergies emerge as a new medical science. This persuaded me to get my Ph.D. in nutrition.

Soon I found local doctors requesting that I see their patients and counsel them on meal management of food allergies. After answering the same questions a few hundred times, I decided to create a booklet with a few recipes and tips on living with food allergies.

I set up a research kitchen, hired a staff, and began to develop hypoallergenic recipes. With more time and practice, I grew increasingly satisfied with the quality of the recipes and was able to create more interesting concoctions.

In my "spare" time I began traveling all over North America, lecturing about food allergies and appearing on various television and radio shows. I received so much mail from people who wanted to share a recipe or offer practical advice on how they managed their diet, I decided to publish a newsletter entitled *Food Allergy and Nutrition Newsletter*.

I received many requests from readers who needed help with their specific food allergies. Using this feedback, I began research on a computer-generated allergy-free diet that would offer recipes and cooking information tailor-made to the person's individual requirements. It took three years of intense work to develop the program. The end result is an extensive notebook similar to the one you will learn to create in Chapter 2.

This book incorporates the information and research developed for the computerized diet, the recipes I have developed over the years for my family and in our research kitchen, and the excellent advice I have received from readers and allergists all over the country. My hope is that it will help you get started on your way to a healthier and happier life. If you have any questions or comments, or would like information about attending a workshop or having me conduct one in your area, write to me and I'll do my best to respond quickly.

Eileen Rhude Yoder, Ph.D.
Medical Diet Systems, Inc.
P.O. Box 1124
Tinley Park, IL 60477-1124

ACKNOWLEDGMENTS

Many people have helped make this book possible, but I'd like especially to thank the following: my family, for their lifelong encouragement and support of anything I undertake; Mel Timmons for his positive outlook on life and motivating me to be the best I can; John Vosatka for his encouragement and patience when I was busy working on the manuscript; Barbara Graubins for her help in typing; Vicki Lansky, my agent, for her guidance; Genoa Shepley, George Gibson, and Lori Snell, my editors, for their constructive suggestions and encouragement; my many readers and patients who have shared their recipes and cooking tips; the staffs at the Orland Park, Palos Park, and Tinley Park libraries for searching for the latest FDA regulations and obtaining other information on food allergies; the board members of the Greater Chicago Chapter of the Asthma and Allergy Foundation for their suggestions and support, and to my many physician friends who have shared their knowledge and experiences with me.

PART ONE

PLANNING

1 · BEGINNING AN ALLERGY-FREE DIET

Have you recently been told by your doctor that you or a family member might have food allergies? Has your doctor recommended that you avoid certain foods for a period of time? Or have you noticed that every time you eat a certain food you feel uncomfortable or even ill? Perhaps you have not identified a particular food that causes problems, but you feel that something you eat causes problems.

If so, this book will help you. An allergy-free diet consists of two steps: the diagnosis or identification of your specific food allergies and the maintenance of your allergy-free diet.

To identify the food or foods you are allergic to, you need to begin an elimination, or avoidance, diet. This is a diet that will enable you to identify the food or foods to which you are allergic by avoiding specific foods that are very often the causes of allergic reactions.

Once you know what your food allergies are, you can tailor your diet to your specific allergy.

THE ELIMINATION DIET

Since most tests for food allergies are not totally accurate, the elimination diet is an important diagnostic tool. If you suspect that you have food allergies, the first step is to visit your physician. Discuss the elimination diet recommended in this book with your doctor and use his guidelines in conjunction with the instructions here. For example, he may want you to avoid other foods in addition to the ten allergens excluded in the elimination diet described in this book.

Based on my research I have found the most common food allergens to be milk, eggs, wheat, sugar (cane and beet), corn, citrus, chocolate, and coffee, as well as additives, preservatives, and colorings. To diagnose your particular food allergies, I recommend that you avoid all of these foods. (This is not as hard as you think; once you have sampled some of the recipes for the elimination diet in Part Two, you may not even miss these foods.)

If your symptoms decrease or disappear by eliminating all of these foods, you are on the right track, and you can introduce foods back to your diet one at a time to determine which ones cause your symptoms. If eliminating all these foods produces no change in your allergies, then you must do some further detective work, so test additional foods such as spices, yeast, beef, and pork. Discuss this with your physician.

Begin your elimination diet by getting your physician's approval. It's also a good idea to ask for guidelines for medications because antihistamines may mask reactions.

Next, read Chapters 1 through 6 to learn how to make the task of beginning and staying on the elimination diet easier. You'll find helpful information on getting organized, shopping for groceries, and cooking.

Browse through the recipes in Part Two and pick out a few you want to try. Also look at the sample menus on pages 55–58 to get some ideas for meals you and your family will enjoy. (It is a good idea if the entire family stays on this diet. It saves time in meal preparation and keeps the person on the allergy-free diet from being tempted to eat the foods he's trying to avoid.)

Stay on the diet for at least two or three weeks until you are symptom free, unless your doctor recommends otherwise, because allergens can remain in the body for one or more weeks.

While on the diet, it is extremely important to remember that even ingesting a slight amount of the allergenic food can produce symptoms, so you must not deviate from the diet, thinking that it won't hurt to have just a taste. If by chance you accidently eat an allergenic food, continue with the diet. However, stay on the diet for two to three weeks more from the date of the ingestion of the suspected allergenic food. Don't become discouraged since this happens to almost everyone!

If at all possible, avoid all contact with these allergens. Just inhaling the odors of some foods can cause allergic symptoms in very sensitive people.

TESTING FOODS

Once your allergy symptoms disappear, you can add foods back to your diet one at a time to see which ones produce reactions. If after several weeks on the elimination diet you still have symptoms, you must test each of the foods you have been eating on the diet. The first step to identifying the food or foods that are still giving you trouble is to check the biological classifications in the appendix. If you are allergic to one food in a classification, you may have a cross-reaction to another food in the same family. For example, if you are allergic to wheat, you may be allergic to corn, rye, or barley and should test each of these separately.

To test a food, for instance corn, eliminate corn in all forms for two to three weeks. Then eat generous portions of pure corn, such as corn on the cob or corn flakes, for three consecutive days. On the first day, eat a small amount (such as one serving of corn flakes) and eat a larger portion on the following days.

If allergic symptoms develop, stop eating the corn. If allergic symptoms do not develop, you can probably assume that corn is acceptable. Continue to eat corn while you test the next food in the same manner. Wait three days before you test the next food since you may have a delayed reaction to corn.

Avoid allergy-causing foods for several months, then retest once more. If symptoms reappear, you'll have to avoid them for several more months. If nothing happens, you can add the food back into your diet. However, eat that food only once every few days so you won't develop an allergy to it again.

THE MAINTENANCE DIET

Once you know what your specific food allergies are, you can begin a maintenance diet. This is a diet specially tailored to your food allergies. You can use the elimination diet recipes in Part Two of this book, adding back those ingredients to which you are not allergic. I have also included recipes that eliminate only one or two of the common allergens. Like the recipes for the elimination diet, many of these recipes can be applied to suit your requirements. Chapter 5 will show you how to modify almost any recipe to avoid particular allergens.

Once you begin the maintenance diet, continue filling out your food diary (see pages 7–8) and other records in your notebook as explained in Chapter 2. After you have determined your food allergies, you might discover (through your food diary) allergies to foods eaten less frequently.

2 · GETTING ORGANIZED

Keeping a careful record of your symptoms can often be the key to success on an allergy-free diet. In fact, a notebook with pertinent information on your particular food allergies can be an invaluable tool. For this purpose I recommend buying a hardcover two- or three-ring binder and dividers with pockets. Keep a separate notebook for each family member who has food allergies.

Your notebook should include the topics listed below, which I will describe separately.

1. Food diary
2. Foods to avoid
3. List of allowed foods, grocery list, and food sources
4. Menus
5. Cooking suggestions and substitutions
6. Recipes and recipe development
7. Miscellaneous

KEEPING A FOOD DIARY

In order to identify the foods that cause you to have allergic reactions, you will find that an accurate record of the foods you eat and your symptoms is indispensable. Keeping a food diary is simple as long as you remind yourself to do it. Just follow these three steps:

1. Draw a chart like the sample food diary below and make copies of the blank chart. Be sure to date and number the pages. Always

carry the day's diet sheet with you and record the foods eaten immediately.

2. Write down everything you eat or drink, including the date and time. List all the ingredients of mixed foods. For example, a chicken salad sandwich might be listed as whole wheat bread, butter, mayonnaise, celery, pepper, and chicken.

3. List all of your symptoms, indicating the degree of severity, when the symptoms occurred, and how long the reaction lasted. You may wish to use a scale of 1 to 4 to indicate the degree of a reaction, with 1 being a very mild reaction and 4 being the worst type of reaction.

Sample Food Diary

Date: 10/5/86

Time	Food/Drink/ Medicine	Time of Symptoms	Symptoms (1–4)
7:00 AM	Tea, rice cereal, milk	9:00 AM	Headache (2) 20 min.
10:00 AM	Apple		No symptom
12:30 PM	Chicken salad sandwich (bread, butter, mayonnaise, chicken, pepper, celery), milk	12:45 PM	Headache (4) 2 hours
		1:45 PM	Hives on face (2) 30 min.
5:30 PM	Steak, baked potato, sour cream, corn	7:00 PM	Headache (4) 2 hours

FOODS TO AVOID

In this part of your notebook you will make a list of all the foods you must eliminate, and include a list of the many derivatives that foods can be processed into or the different words that might be used to describe a product (see Chapter 3).

LIST OF ALLOWED FOODS, GROCERY LIST, AND FOOD SOURCES

Make up a chart of allowed foods and list all the foods you are permitted to eat. For example, if you have rice, include rice cakes, rice crackers, rice cereal, and so on.

Type up a grocery list of foods allowed and make several copies. Put one in your notebook and leave another one in a handy spot so that family members can circle the foods as they are needed. You may want to divide the list into supermarket, health food store, fish market, and fruit stand and list the foods you buy under each section.

Finally, make a chart similar to the one below and keep a list of the new foods you like and where you bought the food item (including mail order items). When you go grocery shopping, you can take the entire notebook with you.

Food Sources

Name of food product: _____

Ingredients: _____

_____

_____

Food bought at: _____

Mail order information: _____

Company manufacturer: _____

Address: _____

City: _____ State: _____ Zip: _____

Telephone: _____

Suggested cooking uses: _____

_____

_____

_____

MENUS

Create a list of menus to keep in your notebook (see samples in Chapter 6). When you plan to go shopping, pick out as many different menus as you wish to shop for and jot down the ingredients. This will help reduce the temptation of eating your former foods.

COOKING SUGGESTIONS AND SUBSTITUTIONS

After reading Chapter 5, you might want to make a list of suggestions for allergy-free cooking and list common food substitutions and ideas for experimenting with a new ingredient as follows:

New Ingredients Worksheet

Mango

· Tried to slice it, rather soft. Perhaps it's overripe. There's not much fruit with the large stone.
· Tried it in a fruit salad with bananas, kiwis, strawberries, and seedless grapes. Delicious!
· Tried it with tuna salad; it's too sweet and mushy. Maybe try it with chicken or sliced over a bland fish. Perhaps it would taste all right sliced over fish and then broiled?
· Put it in the blender and pureed it. Great substitute for applesauce. Because of its sweetness, perhaps it would be good in place of bananas in banana bread recipe?
· The mango sauce darkened; next time try a dash of lemon or pineapple juice to prevent it from darkening.
· Used the exact amount of mango sauce for applesauce in tapioca pudding recipe. Actually has a better, sweeter taste.
· Put it in the blender with water like orange juice. Ugh! Forget it.

Put it in the blender with other fruits and juices:

½ cup orange juice
½ cup apple juice
½ cup diced mango
1 cup crushed ice
1 cup water

Tastes great!

RECIPES

Once you know what foods you're allergic to, you can turn your attention to creating recipes that will suit your personal needs. Rather than constantly flipping back to Chapter 5 on substitutions and suggestions, you may want to keep a record of the new recipes you've created as follows:

Recipe Development Worksheet

~§§~ ORIGINAL RECIPE: Baking-Powder Biscuits

1 cup all-purpose flour
3 teaspoons baking powder
½ teaspoon salt
5 tablespoons oil
¾ cup milk

Preheat the oven to 475°F.

Sift together the dry ingredients. Mix in the oil until finely mixed. Stir in the milk to make a soft dough, which will be a little sticky. Knead on a lightly floured surface for approximately 5 minutes. Press out to ¾ or 1 inch thick. Cut and bake on a greased pan at 475°F. for 10 to 15 minutes until golden brown.

❧ NEW RECIPE: Baking-Powder Biscuits

> 1 1/4 cups potato starch
> 1/4 cup brown rice or barley flour
> 4 teaspoons baking powder
> 1/2 teaspoon salt
> 1/3 cup shortening or oil
> 3/4 to 1 cup oat or sesame milk

Preheat the oven to 475°F.

Sift together the dry ingredients. Mix in the shortening or oil until finely mixed. Stir in the liquid to make a soft dough. Knead on a lightly floured (barley or rice flour) surface for approximately 5 minutes. Press out to 3/4 or 1 inch thick. Cut and bake on a greased pan at 475°F. for 10 to 15 minutes, until golden brown.

MISCELLANEOUS

In this section keep appropriate articles on vitamins, inhalent or chemical allergies, or keep notes on what your doctor suggests to you at each visit or during a phone conversation.

3 · IDENTIFYING ALLERGENS

One of the biggest problems in determining what foods you should avoid is identifying the original source of an ingredient. For example, if you're trying to avoid corn and you scan a packaged food label for this ingredient, you may not find it. However, the label may list a derivative of corn, such as dextrose. The following section will help you decipher labels and avoid foods that include allergens.

WHEAT-CONTAINING FOODS

Many processed foods contain wheat as an ingredient; therefore it is important to know the names of ingredients that indicate the presence of wheat:

all-purpose flour
bran
bread crumbs
bread flour
bulgur
cake flour
cracked wheat flour
cracker meal and crumbs
durum
enriched flour
farina

flour
gluten flour
graham crackers and
    crumbs
graham flour
hydrolyzed vegetable
    protein (hvp)*
malt*
malt syrup*
monosodium glutamate*
pastry flour

*Gluten and/or wheat is often present, but not always.

phosphated flour	wheat germ
semolina	wheat starch
wheat	white flour
wheat flour	whole wheat flour

CORN-CONTAINING FOODS

When looking for corn derivatives on a food label, you should know that corn can be processed into the forms of:

corn syrup
corn meal
corn oil
corn starch

Corn can be further processed into:

modified food starch*	lactic acid
dextrin	sorbitol
fructose	mannitol
maltodextrins	caramel color
dextrose	alcohol

As you can see, this is a formidable list and will require a lot of detection work if you are trying to eliminate corn from your diet. It does not mean, however, that you are automatically allergic to all these items if you are allergic to corn. You may be allergic to some of these products and not to others. Only by going through the elimination diet procedure can you tell for sure which items you are allergic to.

To further help you in the difficult task of avoiding corn, below is a partial list of some of the many foods in which corn may be used:

baby foods	baking powders
bacon	batters for frying
baking mixes	beers

*Modified food starch can also be derived from other ingredients, such as tapioca, potatoes, or wheat.

bleached wheat flours
bourbon and other
    whiskeys
bread and pastries
cakes
candies
carbonated beverages
catsups
cereals
cheeses
chili
chop suey
chow mein
coffee, instant
colas
cookies
confectioners' sugar
cream pies
dextrose
eggnog
fish, prepared and
    processed
foods, fried
French dressing
frostings
fruits, canned and frozen
fruit juices
fruit pies
frying fats
gelatin desserts
gin
ginger ale
glucose and fructose
    products
graham crackers
grape juice
gravies
grits
gums, chewing

hams, cured
Harvard beets
ices
ice creams
jams and jellies
leavening agents and yeasts
liquors
margarines and shortenings
meats, processed and cold
    cuts
milk, in paper cartons
monosodium glutamate
peanut butter and canned
    peanuts
pickles
powdered sugar
puddings and custards
salad dressings
salt
sandwich spreads
sauces for sundaes, meats,
    fish, etc.
sausages
sherbets
soft drinks
spaghetti
soups, thickened, creamed,
    and vegetable
soybean milk
syrups, corn
teas, instant
tortillas
vanillin
vegetables, canned,
    creamed, and frozen
vinegar, distilled
waffles
wines

EGG-CONTAINING FOODS

Eggs are found in most processed foods. Sometimes the presence of eggs is not indicated on the label. For example, egg whites may be brushed on breads, rolls, pretzels, and other baked goods to give a glazed effect. Wine, beer, real root beer, coffee, bouillon, and consommé may be clarified with egg. Some cholesterol-free "egg replacers" may have egg whites as an ingredient.

Egg is present if the label indicates any of the following:

albumin	silico albuminate
globulin	vitellin
ovomucin	ovovitellin
ovomucoid	yolk
powdered or dried egg	livetin

MILK-CONTAINING FOODS

Labels may contain one of the following names if a product contains milk or milk protein:

lactose	lactalbumin
casein	lactoglobulin
caseinate	curds
potassium caseinate	wheys
sodium caseinate	milk solids

Milk has many different proteins, but casein and whey are the most allergy-causing proteins. The whey fraction, which contains lactalbumin and beta lactoglobulin, causes the most reactions. However, after the elimination diet, you should test for both fractions. Individuals who are allergic only to the whey (and not the casein) may be able to tolerate goat's milk since the whey fraction differs from that in cow's milk. Powdered, boiled, or evaporated cow's milk may also be tolerated since the whey protein is changed by the heating process.

Those individuals allergic to whey will have to *avoid*:

> cottage cheese
> soft processed cheeses

Those individuals allergic to whey *may be able to tolerate*:

> hard cheeses (such as Swiss, Edam, Parmesan, Cheddar, Gruyère, and Romano)

Casein remains stable during the heating process, so powdered, evaporated, or boiled milk cannot be consumed. The casein is similar both in goat's milk and cow's milk, so both must be avoided. Even nondairy creamers, imitation processed cheeses, imitation cream cheese, imitation sour cream, and soybean-based ice cream may contain casein. Therefore all labels must be read carefully.

4 · ALLERGY-FREE SHOPPING

Now that you know what foods you must eliminate from your diet, you need to prepare a list of foods you can have. Because you want to avoid your allergens and the additives often present in packaged foods, it is best to shop for foods that are more natural and less processed. When you go to your regular grocery store, buy fresh foods that are not wrapped in plastic bags, heat-sealed plastic, or polystyrene (Styrofoam) in case you are allergic to the plastics. Make sure you read the labels of packaged foods each time you purchase them because product ingredients can change without notice. Also, after the elimination diet, you can try different brands of food products since one brand may be tolerated better than another.

Although you may be able to buy most or all of the foods you need at a grocery store, it's a good idea to locate a well-stocked health food store near your home. Many health food stores offer chemical and additive-free meats, poultry, fish, and produce as well as a variety of ingredients that are difficult to find at a regular supermarket. Some may have personnel who can give you additional suggestions of new ingredients or food products. If you still have trouble locating an ingredient, check the food source list in the back of this book. You may be able to contact the manufacturer directly. Before you make up your own grocery list, read through the section on cooking tips and substitutions, the menus, and recipes to determine which foods make the most sense for your particular diet and tastes.

The following list is a sample of the foods allowed on the elimination diet:

ALLOWED FOODS FOR AN ELIMINATION DIET

*Beverages and
Unsweetened Juices*

Bottled spring water
Apple juice
Apricot nectar
Goat's milk
Grape juice
Pear nectar
Pineapple juice
Tea (including herb teas)
Tomato juice

Condiments and Sweeteners

Apple and grape vinegar
Carob
Coconut (unsweetened)
Date sugar
Honey
Maple syrup or maple
  sugar
Salt and pepper

Herbs and Spices

Allspice
Basil
Bay leaf
Cayenne
Chili powder
Cinnamon
Cloves
Curry powder
Dill
Garlic

Ginger
Oregano
Paprika
Parsley
Rosemary
Sage
Savory

Fruits

Apples
Applesauce
Apricots
Bananas
Blackberries
Blueberries
Cantaloupe and other
  melons
Cherries
Cranberries
Grapes
Dates
Figs
Kiwis
Mangoes
Nectarines
Papayas
Peaches
Pineapple
Plums
Prunes
Raisins
Raspberries
Strawberries
Watermelon

*Cereals, Grains, and
   Thickeners*

Agar
Amaranth
Arrowroot
Barley
Barley flour
Buckwheat
Buckwheat noodles
Gelatin
Oat flour
Oats
Potato flour
Potato starch
Puffed rice cereal
Rice
Rice cakes
Rice flour
Rice crackers
Rice noodles
Rye
Soy flour
Tapioca
Tapioca flour
Xanthan gum

Fresh Meats and Fish

Beef
Chicken
Clam
Duck
Exotic meats such as
   turtle, frog, octopus,
   buffalo
Fish, all types
Lamb

Lobster
Pheasant
Pork
Rabbit
Shrimp
Turkey

Nuts and Raw Seeds

Almonds
Brazil nuts
Cashews
Hazelnuts
Macadamia nuts
Peanuts
Pecans
Pistachios
Sesame seeds
Sunflower seeds
Walnuts
Nut butters

Oils and Fats

Hain safflower margarine
Shedd's spread margarine
Willow Run margarine
Almond oil
Coconut oil
Lamb or beef fat
Walnut oil
Safflower oil
Sesame oil
Soy oil
Sunflower oil

Miscellaneous

Baking powder (cereal free)
Baking soda
Jolly Joan egg replacer
Gelatin
Hain imitation catsup
Hain imitation mayonnaise
Potato chips
Rice cakes
Tuna, packed in water
Vanilla
Vinegar
Wheat-free tamari

Vegetables

Alfalfa
Artichokes
Asparagus
Avocados
Beets
Broccoli
Brussels sprouts
Cabbage
Carrots
Cauliflower
Celery
Chard
Cucumbers
Eggplants
Endive
Escarole
Green beans
Green peas
Green peppers
Kale
Kidney beans
Kohlrabi
Leeks
Lentils
Lettuce, all types
Lima beans
Mushrooms
Navy beans
Onions
Parsnips
Potatoes, white
Potatoes, sweet
Radishes
Rhubarb
Spinach
Split peas
Squash
Tomatoes
Zucchini

To better guide you through your grocery store, I have further elaborated on some of the foods on the previous list. Some of the brand names I mention may not be sold in your area, but other suitable products may be available, so check at your local grocery or health food store for other brands. Always read labels carefully because ingredients can change without notice. If you are not sure how to use a new food, check the cooking tips in Chapter 5.

Apples

Some apples, such as Red Delicious, may be covered with wax and should be avoided. Check with the grocer to find which ones are not waxed or try your local health food store. Use applesauce that is free of preservatives and sugars (such as Mott's Natural Style applesauce). Drink only pure apple juice free of sugar and preservatives (such as After the Fall juices).

Arrowroot

A replacement for cornstarch, it can be located in the spice section of the grocery store. It is also available at health food stores or by mail through Ener-G Foods.

Aspartame

Sold under the brand name Equal, this is a nutritive, high-potency sweetener derived from amino acids that is 200 times sweeter than sugar. It's available at regular grocery stores.

Baking Powder

Buy corn-free baking powder such as Featherweight by Chicago Dietetic Company, available in the diet section of your grocery store.

Barley

You can use an equal amount of barley for wheat. With a small amount of gluten and a mild taste, it is a good substitute for wheat.

Broth/Stock

Most canned broth or stock contains additives, so use only homemade broth or stock (see page 100 for recipes).

Buckwheat

Although buckwheat belongs to the same biological family as rhubarb, it makes a good substitute for wheat. It is available as a flour or as groats. Since the flavor is strong, you might want to combine it with another grain or thickener, or grind white, unroasted whole buckwheat groats into flour.

Carob Powder

As a substitute for chocolate, use equal amounts of carob (El Molino Cara Coa carob powder is 100 percent carob).

Catsup

Because most catsup contains corn and corn sweetener, use Hain imitation catsup, which contains tomato paste, water, honey, cider vinegar, sea salt, and natural spices. Or use Health Valley Catch-Up, which contains tomatoes, water, honey, sea salt, and natural seasonings. (Always check labels as ingredients may change.)

Coconut

Most coconut found in a regular grocery store contains sugar or corn sweeteners and preservatives. Unsweetened coconut is available at health food stores or through Ener-G Foods. To make coconut meal, mix in the blender for a few seconds.

Date Sugar

This sugar is made of finely ground dates with the moisture removed. Although it does not dissolve unless boiled in water for a few minutes, it can be used as a sweetener in beverages, cereals, and desserts. Golden Harvest manufactures a date sugar.

Egg Replacer

Jolly Joan egg replacer and Golden Harvest egg replacer are egg free, but other brands may have egg whites in them. (See pages 37–38 for other egg substitution suggestions.)

Fish

Some fish are dipped into solutions of antibiotics or other preservatives to prevent spoilage. Some fish also contain additives to retain moisture during the freezing process. For example, shrimp may be treated with tripolyphosphate to prevent freezer burn. This chemical does not penetrate the product and can be rinsed off. Ask your grocer about additives.

Flour

Many wheat substitutes are available, such as oats, rice, soy, potato starch, and tapioca starch. Arrowhead Mills, Elam, and Jolly Joan supply oat, rice, and other wheat-substitute flours. (See pages 34–35 for measurement equivalents.)

Fruits

Use fresh fruit or fruit canned in its own juice. Avoid canned fruit with heavy or light syrup as these contain corn, cane, or beet sugar. Dole packs pineapple in its own juice, and Tillie Lewis has fruit packed in unsweetened fruit juice.

Honey

Some commercial honeys come from sugar-fed bees and may cause reactions in people who are sensitive to cane or beet sugar. If possible, buy locally produced honey so you can find out how the bees are fed. See page 39 for directions on substituting honey for sugar.

Juices

Use unsweetened juices such as apple, pineapple, or grape. Avoid lemonade, soft drinks, and other sweetened beverages. After the Fall products include a great variety of acceptable juices.

Maple Sugar

In place of cane or beet sugar, maple sugar can be used. It is more expensive than other sugars but is much sweeter and a smaller amount is required. Order pure maple sugar or maple syrup from American Maple Products or Vermont Country Maple.

Maple Syrup

Use only pure maple syrup such as Old Colony by American Maple Products or Vermont Country Maple. Be sure to read labels carefully; cane or beet is added to some brands.

Margarine

Hain safflower margarine and Willow Run soybean margarine are free of milk and corn.

Mayonnaise

For an egg-free mayonnaise, use Hain eggless mayonnaise. It contains a small amount of lemon juice. It is acceptable on the elimination diet unless you are severely allergic to lemons.

Meats

Do not use processed, smoked, or cured meats (such as hot dogs, bologna, or bacon). They often contain cereal, milk, corn sugar, food coloring, and additives. Do not use frozen turkey that has been basted since it usually contains milk or corn. Fresh meats, fish, and poultry are acceptable.

Milk

Nut milk, soy milk, coconut milk, goat's milk, water, or pure juice can be used in place of cow's milk. Jolly Joan sells soya powder to make soy milk. Jolly Joan has almond nut milk. Jackson-Mitchell, Inc., has fresh, canned, or evaporated Meyenberg goat's milk.

Nuts

If possible, use freshly shelled nuts or raw and unprocessed nuts. Some dry-roasted nuts contain additives and preservatives. Fisher Nut Company and Evons Nuts provide *some* nuts without additives. Read each label carefully.

Oils

On the elimination diet use safflower or sunflower oil in place of corn and combination oils. Hain, Arrowhead Mills, Health Valley, and Hollywood all offer 100 percent pure oils.

Peanut Butter/Nut Butter

Many brands of peanut butter contain sugar and/or oil. You can use peanut butter by Arrowhead Mills (read the label; some contain wheat), Hollywood, or Hain Pure Food. Hain also makes pure nut butters such as cashew butter and almond butter. Arrowhead has sesame tahini made from organically grown sesame seeds.

Paper Goods

If you have an allergy to corn, it's important to note that plastic food wrappers, waxed paper cartons for milk and some juices, paper cups, and wax-coated paper plates are dusted with cornstarch to prevent sticking.

Potato Chips

Use potato chips that are free of additives. Health Valley potato chips contain only potatoes, safflower oil, sunflower oil, and sea salt. Make sure only safflower oil was used in processing.

Rice Cakes

Use Arden rice cakes or Chico San rice cakes as bread substitutes. Hol-Grain makes natural rice wafers.

Salt

Use sea salt, as most packaged salt contains additives and sugar.

Soy Milk

Health Valley makes a liquid soy milk called Soy-Moo. Ener-G Foods has powdered soy milk.

Soy Sauce

Use wheat-free soy sauce such as Tamari-Ya from Health Valley.

Sweeteners

When a recipe calls for a sweetener, use maple sugar, maple syrup, date sugar, rice syrup, or any other acceptable sweetener.

Vanilla

Use fresh vanilla bean if possible.

Vegetables

Discard any outer leaves, peels, skins, or shells to reduce pesticide residue. Some vegetables may be treated with mold inhibitors or fumigated, and red potatoes may be dyed, so check with your grocer.

Xanthan Gum

This is available by mail order from Ener-G Foods; see the list of food sources at the back of the book.

Vinegar

Use a vinegar made from a tolerated food such as grapes or apples.

5 · COOKING SUGGESTIONS AND SUBSTITUTIONS

Although you will be giving up some foods because of allergies, you will most likely want to continue offering meals to your family that you have traditionally prepared. By learning to substitute allergy-free ingredients, you can still enjoy most of your old-time favorites, and with the help of the recipe section in Part Two, you may discover new dishes to savor. At first avoiding an ingredient such as wheat or corn may seem almost impossible until you investigate some of the many substitutes available, such as barley, oats, potato starch, tapioca flour, and soy flour. Of course, there may be some adjustments to make in the amount of alternative flour you substitute or perhaps in the cooking time or temperature, but with a little effort, you'll soon be an expert at wheat-free or corn-free cooking.

You will have to experiment with new ingredients and perhaps even create new recipes. If you and your family think of this as a sort of cooking adventure, you will find it easier to overcome some of the frustrations caused by the changes in your dietary habits. Some substitutions will not affect the taste of a new recipe, but others will produce a different taste, which may take some time to get used to. You may even make some changes in your diet that better suit your tastes.

In this chapter you will learn about the many different substitutes available for most common food allergens and how to adjust almost any recipe to match your needs and tastes. It's a good idea to keep experimenting with different substitutes because it's possible to develop allergies to new foods that are eaten too frequently. It will also help you make adjustments more easily when you travel or eat in restaurants.

WHEAT-FREE COOKING

Wheat and other grains—corn, rice, oats, rye, and barley—are the staples of the human diet. Because most Americans eat wheat on a daily basis, avoiding it is difficult. Wheat flour contains gluten, which helps to give a good structural framework to breads and cakes. Other flours such as rye contain little or no gluten. Commercial bakeries generally combine these other flours with wheat flour to make bread, for instance. In most cases, you'll have to make your own baked goods to avoid wheat (or go to a health food store that special orders wheat-free bread). Read the labels carefully; even soybean-based baked goods or rye and potato breads may contain some wheat to help them rise.

Baked products made without wheat flour tend to be heavier and more crumbly than those made with wheat flour. This difference is most noticeable in breads and cakes.

Oats, barley, rice, and rye can be suitable substitutions if you have a wheat allergy (see pages 34–35 for exact replacement proportions). Oats tend to produce a somewhat sticky feel in the mouth. Rice flour gives a distinct graininess to baked goods. Rye flour has a dark color and distinctive flavor. Rye baked goods are more compact and heavier than wheat products because of the low amount of gluten. After the elimination diet you might try corn flour, which produces a heavy, crumbly baked good since it is gluten free. Barley has a mild flavor and contains a slight amount of gluten, making it a nice substitute for wheat.

Because barley and other grains are closely related to wheat, some individuals are allergic to them. If during the elimination diet you discover you have cross-reactions to other grains, you can use nongrain flour alternatives such as buckwheat, which is not a grain but a member of the rhubarb family. It makes acceptable pancakes and breads but is not a good thickener. Dark buckwheat flour, which is ground from roasted buckwheat groats, has a very strong flavor, so you might want to mix it with another nongrain flour if possible. White buckwheat flour has a mild, mellow flavor. It is made from unroasted whole groats and can be ground in a blender.

Nuts, seeds, or beans are good substitutes for anyone allergic to grains. When ground into meal, they may be substituted for any flour. Simply put ¼ cup of nuts at a time into a blender and using on/off turns, briefly process to a fine powder. (Watch carefully; if you process too long, you'll end up with nut butter instead.)

Thickeners

Most grain flours will act as thickeners in place of wheat, but there are also several nongrain alternatives. Potato flour is useful as a thickener in sauces. When mixed with soy flour, potato flour also makes acceptable baked goods. Tapioca flour is the starch made from the fleshy root of the manioc or cassava plant. It is best used as a thickener or for small cookies.

Starchy vegetables may be used as a thickener for gravies, soups, or stews by first cooking and then mashing or pureeing. Vegetable flour can be made out of squash, pumpkin, yams, potatoes, or carrots. Peel and cut into chunks, then dry in a very slow oven or dehydrator. Grind to a fine powder.

When using alternative flours to thicken, dissolve first in cold water to prevent lumps, just as you would cornstarch.

Noodle Substitutes

Noodles can be made from scratch using such wheat-free substitutes as amaranth flour, buckwheat flour, rice flour, or oat flour. (See Oat Noodle recipe on page 170.)

Although difficult to find, there are wheat-free noodles available through mail order or health food stores. Eden Foods makes noodles with 100 percent buckwheat flour, for example. See the appendix on food sources for further information.

Other Grain Substitutes

Amaranth is not in the grain family but in the pyrethrum family. It can be used alone as a flour substitute or mixed with other grains. Amaranth was the primary source of food for the Aztecs some 3,000 years ago. In order to control the Aztec population, Cortez ordered all the amaranth destroyed. It was recently rediscovered growing wild in Central America and was brought back to the United States. Since it is still a relatively new crop, only a small amount is grown here at present. A good substitute for those who must avoid wheat, amaranth is high in protein, and when mixed with grain or a food containing thiamine (such as pork), it provides 100 percent of the essential amino acids.

Quinoa pronounced (*keen-wa*) is similar to grains but is not in the grain family. It is in the Chenopodium Family, which is closely related to beets and spinach. Like amaranth, it was recently discovered growing in South America. Uncooked, it looks like sesame seeds. It needs to be rinsed several times to remove the bitter protective coating. It cooks like rice and has a pleasant crunch. Quinoa can be used in place of any grain, in casseroles, cold salads, or desserts. It is a complete protein and contains amino acids similar to whole dried milk. Since quinoa must be washed, however, it does not make a good flour substitute. Quinoa and amaranth can be ordered from the Illinois Amaranth Company (see the appendix that lists food sources for address).

Wheat Substitutions

Various flours in the following quantities can be substituted for 1 cup wheat flour:

> 1 cup corn flour
> ¾ cup coarse cornmeal
> ¾ cup cornstarch
> ⅝ cup potato flour*
> ⅞ cup buckwheat*
> ⅞ cup rice flour*
> 1⅓ cups ground rolled oats*
> 1⅛ cups oat flour*
> ¾ cup soybean flour or other bean flour*
> 1 cup barley*
> 1 cup millet*

*Suitable for the elimination diet.

1 cup tapioca flour*
1¼ cup rye flour*
¾ cup potato starch*
½ cup ground nuts or seeds*

These flour combinations are equivalent to 1 cup wheat flour:

½ cup rye flour + ⅓ cup potato flour*
⅓ cup rye flour + ⅝ cup rice flour*
1 cup soy flour + ¾ cup potato flour*
⅝ cup rice flour + ⅓ cup potato flour*
½ cup cornstarch + ½ cup rye flour
½ cornstarch + ½ cup potato flour

To replace 1 tablespoon wheat flour as a thickener for sauces, gravies, and puddings, use one of the following:

½ tablespoon cornstarch
½ tablespoon potato starch*
½ tablespoon rice flour*
½ tablespoon arrowroot*
2 teaspoons quick-cooking tapioca*
2 tablespoons uncooked rice*
½ tablespoon bean flour or nut flour*
½ tablespoon gelatin*
1 tablespoon tapioca flour*
1 egg
1 teaspoon xanthan gum*

Spaghetti and noodle substitutes (see package labels for proportions and cooking times):

Chinese bean threads (mung beans)*
Rice*
Rice noodles*
Corn noddles
Oat noodles*
Buckwheat noodles*

*Suitable for the elimination diet.

Tips on Wheat-Free Cooking

- Wheat-free products should be baked at a lower temperature and for a longer period of time.
- Many substitute flours, such as soy flour, have a higher fat content than wheat, so slightly decrease the amount of shortening in each recipe.
- When combining flours, sift several times to make sure the flours are well mixed.
- To help improve the texture of baked goods, add an extra ½ teaspoon baking power per cup of flour.
- Refrigerating dough for half an hour before baking helps improve the texture and flavor.
- Since most wheat-free baked foods will crumble, it is best to make foods with smaller surface areas, such as cupcakes instead of cakes. Use small loaf pans for quick breads. Do not pour the dough higher than 2 to 4 inches because the bottom will not cook thoroughly.
- A fast, convenient way to prepare baked goods is to buy wheat-free ready mixes by such companies as Ener-G Foods or Richard's Natural Foods.
- After the elimination diet, substitute crushed cornflakes or Rice Krispies for breading foods.
- Xanthan makes a great thickener in place of wheat, gelatin, or eggs. Add 1 teaspoon to a gluten-free recipe to hold the baked good together. It also makes a creamy smooth sauce and thickens puddings, salad dressings, and gravies. Xanthan gum has to be specially ordered but it's well worth the effort. (See Ener-G Foods under Food Sources.)

CORN-FREE COOKING

Corn-derived products are probably the most difficult ingredients to eliminate completely from a diet because they are found in so many prepared foods. Because of the widespread use of corn, the best way to avoid it is by preparing your foods at home. Although corn is present in many packaged foods, you can easily cook without it.

Below are a few corn-free cooking tips.

- Substitute other starches, such as tapioca flour, rice flour, arrowroot, or potato starch to thicken foods.
- Use corn-free baking powder, such as Featherweight cereal-free baking powder.
- Maple syrup, maple sugar, honey, cane or beet sugar (not during the elimination diet), or date sugar can replace corn syrup.
- Corn-free oil such as safflower oil, coconut oil, and sunflower oil is easy to find and just as flavorful.
- Use sea salt since regular salt contains dextrose, a corn derivative that is used to stabilize the iodine.

EGG-FREE COOKING

There are many ways to substitute eggs in a recipe, depending on what you are making. In cooking, eggs act as a binder, leavener, and thickener. If you do not use a leavening ingredient, the product will be heavier. It is best to use the following substitutes in recipes calling for one to two eggs only.

- Use an egg substitute such as Jolly Joan egg replacer or Golden Harvest egg replacer. Other brands may have egg whites in them.
- Mashed bananas and apricot puree add flavor and act as both a binder and thickener in place of eggs in quick breads, cakes, cookies, or other sweets. Use 2 tablespoons pureed fruit for each egg called for in the recipe. Also, 2 tablespoons of pureed vegetables can replace an egg in soups, sauces, and other dishes.
- To bind or thicken fruit desserts, use 1 teaspoon dry, unflavored gelatin mixed with 2 tablespoons liquid to replace one egg.
- Since baked goods without eggs crumble easily, use smaller pans. For example, make cupcakes instead of a cake, or muffins instead of bread. Xanthan gum is excellent for holding baked goods together. Use 1 teaspoon per recipe.
- To help leaven a baked good, add an extra ½ teaspoon

egg-free baking powder for each egg called for in a recipe along with another egg substitute to bind or thicken.

· For thickening cream dishes and sauces, add extra flour, cornstarch, or xanthan gum.

· To enhance the flavor of egg-free cookies or cakes, add extra ingredients like raisins, nuts, coconut, seeds, or spices.

· Since homemade egg-free mayonnaise tastes more like flour and vinegar mixed together, it is best to avoid recipes calling for mayonnaise or else try Hain imitation mayonnaise. (Always read the label first to verify ingredients.)

MILK-FREE COOKING

Milk is difficult to avoid when buying prepared foods, but it is easy to replace in recipes. Substitute an equal amount of other liquids for milk in recipes as follows:

· Try fruits or fruit juices in place of milk on hot cereal.

· Use fruit juice, vegetable juice, pureed fruits, or pureed vegetables in place of milk in such recipes as quick breads, cookies, or cakes. Add an extra tablespoon of shortening to the recipe.

· If you use soy milk, its flavor can be improved by adding ½ to 1 teaspoon vanilla for each cup and, if desired, a teaspoon of honey. Chill before serving.

· Rich's Coffee Rich has a nice flavor; however, it is very high in calories.

· Use fresh goat's milk. You can also buy goat's milk powdered or canned evaporated.

· You can make delicious banana, nut, or oat milk (recipe, page 59) or buy nut milk from Ener-G Foods (see Food Sources).

· In sauces and gravies, use pure meat, chicken, or vegetable broth as a substitute for milk.

· Fry foods in safflower or another allowed oil instead of butter or margarine.

· For a great thick chocolate shake, put xanthan gum and

milk substitute in a blender and mix well. Add chocolate or carob plus the allowed sweetener.
· To make sour cream, mix ½ cup allowed starch with ¾ cup water, soybean milk, or goat's milk, and stir in ¼ cup vinegar.

SUGAR-FREE COOKING

You will notice that some of the recipes in this book call for a sweetener but do not specify which sweetener. You may use any type of natural sweetener unless you are on the elimination diet, when you must avoid corn sweeteners and cane and beet sugar.

Honey requires a little more adjustment when substituted for sugar. Use the same amount of honey as sugar or decrease by one-quarter to one-half, depending on the type of honey and your preferences. When baking with honey, you must account for its extra density. Each cup of honey or any syrup contains approximately ¼ cup of liquid. Therefore, deduct ¼ cup of liquid for every cup of honey or syrup being substituted. Add approximately ¼ teaspoon baking soda to whatever is called for in the recipe to neutralize the acids.

Also lower the oven temperature by 25 degrees since honey caramelizes at a low temperature. Otherwise your baked good will become too brown on top before the inside is done.

You can combine honey with other sweeteners for a variety in taste. Also try different brands of honey. Lighter colored honeys, such as clover, sage, and alfalfa, are milder and are good for general cooking, alone or blended.

Buy honey from a source you can trust, as some large producers feed their bees sugar water.

If honey crystalizes (a natural occurrence), it can be reliquefied by simply placing the container in a pan of hot water for several minutes.

Date sugar is produced from ground, dried dates. It is not absorbed like regular sugar, making its use limited. For best results, use recipes specifically written for the use of date sugar. Date sugar can be dissolved by boiling it in water for 5 minutes. It is also good sprinkled on French toast or cereal.

Maple syrup and maple sugar can be used in place of sugar. You may want to use half the amount since it has a stronger flavor than white sugar, and decrease maple syrup proportionately as you would for honey.

Corn and barley malt is a syrup naturally processed from 60 percent sprouted barley and 40 percent corn. After the elimination diet, use an equal amount in place of either honey or maple syrup. It is not as sweet as these two are, so you may want to combine the malt with honey or maple syrup.

Malt extract is a pure malt syrup and can be used as you would honey. Rice syrup can be used equally in place of honey but will not be as sweet. (Available at health food stores and through mail order.)

Fruit syrups can be made by boiling pure, unsweetened fruit juices (such as pear or apple) down to one-fourth or one-third of the original volume. This syrup is as sweet as maple syrup and may be substituted in equal amounts for honey or maple syrup. In addition, fruit syrups are only half the cost of maple syrup or honey.

Aspartame (brand name Equal) is a new sugar substitute; only a minute amount is needed in a recipe. It cannot be used during prolonged baking or cooking because its amino acids break down with heat, causing a loss of sweetness. Special recipes have been developed and can be ordered through the manufacturer, Searle Lab. (Look at the box of Equal for address and other information.) Although it contains a mixture of ingredients, including lactose, it might be better to use Equal in place of sugar.

CHOCOLATE-FREE COOKING

It's rather easy to avoid the chocolate in candy, cakes, frosting, ice cream, and cookies since these food products are well labeled, but you also have to watch out for cocoa, cola, and karaya gum (often listed as vegetable gum), which are closely related to chocolate.

Carob can be used as a substitute for chocolate. However, since it is in the legume family, it may cause an allergy. Substitute an equal amount of carob for chocolate. Oven temperatures should be lowered 25 degrees for baking.

6 · CHILDREN AND FOOD ALLERGIES

If your child is on the elimination diet, you should explain the diet to him before you begin. You and he might prepare the foods together. So that your child better understands this diet and willingly participates in it, make a "contract" stating that he understands why he must be on this diet, that he is willing to stay on it, and what rewards he will earn. Create a little "reward book" in which you write down what foods he eats. Every time he eats an allergy-free meal, give him a sticker or star to place in the book. After he receives so many stickers, he earns a reward.

Make up a notebook for your child as described in Chapter 2. If your child is spending a night with a friend, he and his notebook and pajamas can go off together. The friend's parents can consult the notebook to determine what foods are safe for dinner, snacks, and breakfast the next morning. They can also quickly tell which foods and ingredients to avoid.

You may also want to fill out a form similar to the one on the next page and tape it to the inside front cover of the notebook.

SCHOOL LUNCHES

Additives, preservatives, and unwanted ingredients in packaged and prepared foods can make it very difficult for a child with allergies to eat convenience foods or school lunches. To manage a diet for the allergic child at school, you may have to send along substitute foods. During the trial elimination diet, you will almost certainly have to send all foods and snacks.

41

PLANNING

Emergency Medical Information

Child's name: _____ Age: _____

Address: _____

Telephone: _____

Mother's place of work: _____

Address: _____

Telephone: _____

Father's place of work: _____

Address: _____

Telephone: _____

Physician: _____

Address: _____

City: _____ State: _____ Zip: _____

Telephone: _____

Hospital: _____

Address: _____

Telephone: _____

Foods to avoid: (list)

_____

_____

_____

Medications: (include amount and times to be given)

_____

_____

_____

Children spend a major part of their day at school. It is important that your child and the school staff clearly understand your child's diet needs. You must help the staff to realize that your child has to adhere totally to the elimination diet if it is to be successful.

To make matters easier for everyone involved, ask for a conference with the principal, the teacher(s), the school nurse, and someone from the cafeteria service. Make sure that provisions are made to inform substitute classroom teachers of the diet requirements. Make a list of everything to which your child is allergic. Give copies to the staff. If your child's diet permits use of some cafeteria food, ask the cafeteria staff worker to let your child know what foods he may have. Make a separate list of the allergic reactions your child might experience, such as a sudden earache, and give it to the staff.

Your child's classmates should also be told about his allergies so that they don't tempt or pressure him to eat the wrong foods. A great way to overcome other children's attitudes that your child is "different" is to go to the classroom and simply explain what allergies are. Of course, a tasty batch of homemade "allergy" cookies will convince the children that your child is actually no different than other children.

Lunch Ideas

All of the following suggestions are suitable for the elimination diet. You'll find recipes for many of them in Part Two.

- Homemade bread, rice cakes, or crackers with slices of meat or other fillings such as tuna, roast beef, pork, lamb, chicken, fish, peanut butter, nut butter, and homemade jelly
- Salads: chicken salad, tossed salad, turkey salad, or fruit salad
- Cookies, fruit bars, cupcakes, pie, or cake
- Fruit leathers, granola
- Fruit: mixed or separate, either fresh, frozen, or canned (without sweetener), apples, bananas, pears, peaches, plums, nectarines, mangoes, grapes, cherries, watermelon, cantaloupe, pineapple, apricots, and strawberries

- Potato chips made with safflower oil
- Vegetables: celery, carrots, lettuce, sliced tomatoes, cucumbers, radishes, green peppers, cauliflower, mushrooms
- Individual cans or boxes of unsweetened fruit juices
- Homemade soups

Forgotten Lunches

In case your child forgets to bring a lunch to school, send a few canned food items in advance that can be stored in his locker. The school may request that the food be in sealed glass containers or cans to avoid insects.

Some suggestions for foods that can be stored at school:

- Starkist packages a 3½-ounce serving of tuna in water with a pop-top lid. It is sold three cans to a package.
- Look for individual servings of fruits canned in their own juice or water.
- A few brands of potato chips made with safflower oil are packaged in individual servings.
- Rice cakes can be wrapped individually and kept a long time. They contain no preservatives or additives.
- Nuts and seeds without additives or preservatives can be kept in small glass jars or bought in small individual packages.
- Small individual cans or paper cartons of unsweetened juice will store a long time.

Tips for preparing lunches:

- Put together a week's worth of sandwiches at a time. Spread each slice of bread with allowed margarine so they won't become soggy, add the meat or spread, wrap, label, and freeze. Take the sandwich out in the morning and it will thaw before lunch. Put lettuce and tomato in a separate bag.
- Package and freeze small quantities of meat, poultry, or spread and put packages into the lunch box at the last minute.

- Freeze individual cartons or boxes of pure fruit juice. They will thaw out but still be cold by lunch time. (Before packing frozen juice into a paper bag, put it in a separate plastic bag. Otherwise moisture on the outside of the juice container may cause the bag to rip.)
- If possible, make lunch the night before to avoid early morning hassles. Right after dinner is a great time to pack lunch. Put leftovers in small containers and refrigerate or freeze immediately.

EATING AWAY FROM HOME

Before you and your child go to a restaurant, plan ahead. Most restaurants do not offer specialized allergy-free menus. At some fine restaurants knowledgeable chefs can cater to your family's individual needs. Remember that the same dish at two different restaurants may have different ingredients. Always ask before you order anything.

National chain restaurants generally use the same type of ingredients throughout their restaurants. Inquire about the foods at these various chain restaurants so that you will know which ones are acceptable. If eating out at a restaurant or other social gathering is awkward for you because you are worried about your child eating something he is allergic to, call up the restaurant in advance to see if they can accommodate your child's needs.

Traveling by Car

An overnight stay might require bringing along whatever foods are necessary. Traveling by car can be enjoyable for your family if you plan ahead and have the room to take along canned and refrigerated foods. Even if you plan to eat at restaurants while you travel, you may still need to bring along additional foods. Restaurants would rather have you bring your own foods to substitute than see your child have a reaction to the food.

Below are some suggested foods that you might take along when you travel while you or your child is on the elimination diet:

- Rye crackers, such as Ry-Krisps
- Small cans of unsweetened fruit juices
- Nut butters or peanut butter
- Seeds and nuts
- Fruit, either fresh or canned in its own juice, such as unsweetened applesauce or pineapple
- Milk substitute, such as soy milk, evaporated or powdered goat's milk, or nut milk
- Dried fruits (Some dried fruits are preserved with sulfur, so check the label. Honey-coated fruits may also have been treated with other preservatives. Dark raisins are sun dried, without preservatives, whereas golden light raisins are preserved with sulfur.)
- Sweeteners (Try Equal or pure maple sugar granules, which come in a small plastic shaker.)
- Homemade muffins and breads
- Fresh vegetables
- Plain canned fish or meat, such as tuna packed in water or chicken in chicken broth

Traveling by Plane

Although airlines do not yet offer allergy-free menus, most will accept special meal requests. You will need to specify what your child can and cannot eat and your request must be made at least twenty-four hours in advance of your flight.

If your child has severe food allergies, you may find it more satisfactory to bring his own meal with him or to plan on eating beforehand.

FOOD ALLERGIES AND HOLIDAYS

Birthdays

Putting together a birthday party for a child with food allergies requires some extra planning. Although traditional birthday and holiday foods are allergen-containing, you can make delicious allergy-free substitutes so that your child can enjoy a special occasion without suffering a food reaction. (Remember, it's crucial to maintain the diet at all times, especially during the elimination diet.)

If your child wants traditional cake and ice cream, that's fine. Just make the cake yourself (see Chapter 16 for recipes) or find a baker who will follow your recipe. Perhaps a friend will make an allergen-free cake for the child as a present.

Many cakes made without wheat flour or eggs are quite crumbly. Don't try a two-layer cake. The batter will produce great cupcakes that can be individually decorated. Or you can make cupcakes for everyone, using a regular recipe for the guests and an allergy-free recipe for your child.

Easter

Traditional Easter goodies—colored eggs, chocolate bunnies, and jelly beans—may have to be avoided by children with food allergies. Parents can help their allergic children celebrate a traditional Easter by being inventive. Substitute plastic eggs filled with small trinkets such as balloons, coins, or jewelry. If the child is allergic to the plastic, make a paper ball. Cut colorful paper into thin strips and wrap the paper around small trinkets. Continue adding trinkets and wrapping the paper around them until you have a large ball.

So that your child won't miss out on decorating Easter eggs, take a raw egg and puncture each end with a needle. Blow out the egg and rinse the inside of the shell a few times, then decorate with markers, paints, and crayons. If your child is severely allergic to eggs, you can buy plastic eggs and paint them. Make tasty Easter surprises out of maple sugar or make cookies in the shape of bunnies or eggs.

Halloween

Since Halloween involves leaving home to go trick-or-treating, it presents special problems. Tell your neighbors about your children's allergies and ask them if they could provide something suitable for your child. Either a snack (such as fruit or allergen-free cookies) or small trinkets such as pencils, balloons, or money would delight any child.

If possible, have a Halloween party at home or plan a special Halloween party for children with food allergies. Have each family bring a favorite treat as well as the recipe. The children then decide for themselves what they can eat.

Christmas

For most people, the days between Thanksgiving and the New Year are filled with family get-togethers and holiday party celebrations. Although this can be a difficult time for the person with food allergies, careful planning and preparation can free you from unexpected allergic reactions. Here are a few suggestions to help you during this busy time of the year:

- Plan your holiday menus well in advance.
- Order special ingredients early.
- Prepare as much food ahead of time as possible and freeze. Cookies, breads, and cakes freeze well and thaw rapidly if unexpected company arrives. Have a few meals frozen and ready to heat for overwhelmingly hectic days.
- Make foods that are suitable for entertaining, such as Oatmeal Bread, Pecan Balls, or Carob Candy. (See recipes, pages 66, 135, and 147).

FOOD ALLERGIES AND ILLNESSES

Children suffer from an occasional illness for which your physician might prescribe a soft or liquid diet. Generally, soft diets consist of puddings, soups, and ice cream, while a liquid diet restricts intakes to gelatins, carbonated beverages, juices, and broths.

During an illness, an individual's allergic threshold is often lowered, and food preparation becomes increasingly important. Not only must the child's nutritional needs be met, but also adequate fluid intake (hydration) must be maintained.

The following is a listing of allergen-free substitutes/alternatives for foods commonly taken as part of a liquid or soft diet. Recipes will be found in Part Two.

- For carbonated beverages, substitute pure fruit juices and Perrier water, or mixed fruit juices.
- For ice cream and popsicles, substitute homemade sherbets and ice creams, frozen fruits, and juices.
- For packaged puddings and gelatin desserts, substitute homemade puddings and gelatin desserts, applesauce, and pureed fruits.
- For soups and cereals, substitute homemade broths, cream of rice, and cream of buckwheat.

PART TWO

RECIPES

7 · MEAL PLANNING AND MENUS

Most of the recipes in this part are for the elimination diet; that is, they exclude wheat, eggs, milk, sugar (cane and beet), citrus, chocolate, and coffee, plus additives, preservatives, and colorings. Once you have tested these foods and know which ones you are allergic to, you can use these same recipes and add the ingredients that do not produce allergic reactions. Many of the recipes have suggestions for adding back foods. You will also find recipes that eliminate some, but not all, ten allergens. Most of these can also be modified for your particular allergies. For appropriate substitutions and equivalent measures, see Chapter 5.

TIMESAVING TECHNIQUES

To save time, make breads, muffins, pancakes, cookies, and "TV dinners" in advance of serving. Divide the foods into individual or meal-size portions and double wrap with aluminum foil. Label, date, and freeze.

If you are freezing a casserole, line the baking dish with aluminum foil and pour in the casserole. Cover the casserole dish with a sheet of foil and fold the edges together, sealing tightly and pressing the air out. Label, date, and freeze. When frozen solid, lift from the pan and return the frozen package to the freezer. To serve, preheat the oven to approximately 425°F and place the foil package in its original pan. Bake, covered, for approximately 35 minutes. Remove the top sheet of foil and bake an additional 10 to 15 minutes, until the sauce is hot and bubbly.

If the casserole includes meat, precooking the meat will eliminate greasiness and shorten the reheating time.

When reheating individual portions in a microwave, remove the foil and put the food on a microwave-safe plate. Cover with plastic wrap, turning back one edge to vent. Microwave on high power for 4 to 7 minutes, or until thoroughly heated.

Since you will need to spend more time in the kitchen preparing special allergy-free foods, try to prepare a few meals at one time. For example, prepare double the amount of food you need for a meal and freeze the remainder. When planning your menus, create meals in which you can use the same foods. For example, when coring apples for fresh applesauce at breakfast or lunch, core extra apples for an Apple Crisp dessert. When shredding potatoes for hash browns, shred extra for Potato Pancakes. Store the potatoes in water with a small amount of ascorbic acid (vitamin C).

While in the kitchen preparing your regular meal, make a sauce or soup that needs to simmer for a long time. For example, spaghetti sauce takes only a few minutes to prepare but needs to simmer for a few hours. If you want to use hamburger in the sauce, plan a casserole or dish for your evening meal that uses browned hamburger. Brown the hamburger for both meals and divide it for the casserole and spaghetti sauce.

An electric slow cooker is a great time-saver. Just before bedtime, add whole grains and the necessary water and cook all night on low. Breakfast will be ready to eat in the morning. Or cook some meat for breakfast. After breakfast, place some vegetables on top of the meat and let them simmer until lunch or dinner. You can also make soups, chili, or beef stew and have it ready to eat any time of the day.

Set aside one day a week or so and prepare the basic "staples" for your diet. For example, make oat noodles first (this allows time for the noodles to dry before freezing), and then mix up granola (the grain needs to be heated). Make up several loaves of bread, slice, wrap each piece individually (or place waxed paper between the slices), and freeze. You can also mix the dry ingredients together for pancakes, muffins, or biscuits. Later all you have to do is add the liquid and cook.

Freeze nuts in their shells or remove the shells to save space in freezer. Frozen nuts can last for two years.

When grinding nuts and seeds or shredding coconut, prepare a large amount (such as 4 to 6 cups). Buy large amounts of fruits at one time, such as bananas or apples, and eat them as they ripen. When the apples will no longer keep, peel, slice, and puree in a blender or food processor and freeze in half-pint containers. Packed in a lunch box, the apple puree will thaw out by noon. If you like, you can add chopped nuts, seeds, coconut, or dried fruit to the pureed fruit. If you have extra bananas, peel and freeze some of them whole. When frozen, you can roll them in chopped nuts or make the recipe for Frosty Freezer Treats.

MENUS

In developing the menu suggestions for the elimination diet, I have put together foods that complement one another in flavor and in nutritional value. Some of the menus may be more ambitious than you like, and you may not want to serve all of the foods listed at one meal. I have provided them simply to get you started and encourage your own inspirations.

Menus for the Elimination Diet

Breakfast

Toasted Oatmeal Bread*
  with Strawberry Jam*
  and Nut Butter*
Hot carob cocoa made
  with Nut Milk*
Ground beef burgers
Banana Pineapple Cooler*
Fresh homemade
  applesauce
Potato Pancakes*
Pure pork sausage

Meal Planning Tips

Make Oatmeal Bread
ahead of time, slice and
wrap separately, and
freeze.

Grate potatoes the night
before and store in a container filled with water to
prevent them from turning
dark.

*Recipes included.

RECIPES

Breakfast (continued)

Apple Oatmeal*
Turkey burgers
Grape juice

Fresh cantaloupe
Apple Rice Betty*
Nut Milk*

Sliced fresh peaches
Peanut Butter Rice
   Muffins*
Broiled chicken breast

Soya Shake*
Fresh sliced fruit
Hasty Pudding*
Pork patties

Cantaloupe and watermelon balls
Apple Cinnamon Crunchy
   Granola*
Broiled fish

Meal Planning Tips

Use fresh ground turkey
and add your own allowed
seasonings, as the turkey
tastes very bland.

Squeeze pineapple juice
onto the peaches to keep
them from turning brown.

Lunch

Tropical Shake*
Tomato Soup*
Carrot Bread* with sliced
   turkey and Eggless
   Mayonnaise*
Pecan Balls*

Banana Shake*
Chicken Soup*
Oatmeal Crackers*
Tuna Salad Luau*
Carob Candy*

Meal Planning Tips

Cook fresh turkey; do not
use packaged lunch meat.

*Recipes included.

56

Lunch *(continued)*

Chicken and Potato Soup*
Broiled Burgers*
Catsup*
Potato chips
Applesauce
Raisin Nut Cookies*

Spaghetti sauce served
  over China Bowl Rice
  Sticks*
Stuffed Mushrooms*
Sunflower Salad*

Minestrone Soup*
Carrot and celery sticks
Molded Fruit Gelatin*
Rice Baking-Powder
  Biscuits*

Pea Soup*
Banana Honey Salad*
Radishes
Rye Crisp*

Meal Planning Tips

Buy potato chips pro-
cessed with safflower oil.

Rice stick noodles are
available at health food
stores or in the Oriental
food section.

The soup tastes better
after a day or so.

Ry-Krisp bought at the
supermarket can be substituted for the recipe Rye
Crisp.

Dinner

Fruit Melon Shake*
Pork Chop Spanish Rice*
Braised Celery*
Molded Fruit Gelatin*
Almond Crescents*

Chicken or Turkey Loaf*
Mashed potatoes
Eggplant with Tomato*
Biscuits*

Meal Planning Tips

Mix all the dry ingredients
together for the biscuits
and cut in the shortening.
Store in the refrigerator
until ready to bake, then
add the liquid.

*Recipes included.

RECIPES

<table>
<tr><td>Dinner (continued)</td><td>Meal Planning Tips</td></tr>
<tr><td>

Pineapple Pork Chops
  with Rice*
Tossed salad with French
  Dressing*
Green beans
Fruity Spice Cake*

Quick Savory Meat Loaf*
Baked potato
Steamed or Maple
  Carrots*
Cranberry Relish*
Watermelon Sherbet*

Broiled Burgers*
Oriental Tomato Skillet*
Fruity Rice Pudding*

Chicken Supreme* with
  Mushroom Sauce*
Green Beans with
  Almonds*
Banana Cake*

</td><td>

Wrap extra cooked
Chicken Supreme with
sauce in individual portions
and freeze, or make up
"TV dinners." All these
foods freeze well. Great
for those really hectic
days.

</td></tr>
<tr><td>

Fried fish with Tartar
  Sauce*
Confetti Rice*
Tossed salad with oil and
  vinegar
Pumpkin Pecan Pie*
French onion soup
Baked Chicken with To-
  mato Rice Stuffing*
Strawberry Pie*

</td><td>

Make up your own dress-
ing of oil and vinegar and
add your favorite allowed
seasonings.

Freeze extra soup in ice
cube trays and store in a
plastic bag. Take out sev-
eral cubes and heat for a
cup of soup.

</td></tr>
</table>

*Recipes included.

8 · BEVERAGES

Living without cow's milk seems to be one of the most difficult adjustments an allergic individual must deal with.

In our research kitchen we have developed an exciting and unusual array of great-tasting beverages. You'll hardly notice the absence of a glass of milk at mealtime.

You'll find such tempting recipes as Banana Pineapple Cooler, Coconut Milk, Fresh Melon Shake, Banana Peach Drink, and Kiwifruit Spritzer. In fact, by adding nuts, soy powder, or other high-protein foods, you'll have a quick, nutritious breakfast.

❧ NUT, BANANA, OR OAT MILK*

Use one of the following:

> ⅓ cup nuts or seeds (cashews, walnuts, sliced almonds, sunflower seeds, sesame seeds)
> OR 2 teaspoons rolled oats
> OR ½ small banana

Combine the nuts, seeds, oats, or banana and 1 cup water in a blender on highest speed until smooth. Use instead of cow's milk for baking and on cereals. Banana milk is delicious on cereal but must be used immediately.

Makes approximately 1¼ cups.

* Suitable for the Elimination Diet

⋖§§⋗ COCONUT MILK*

Meat of 1 fresh coconut, cut into pieces
Liquid from 1 fresh coconut
2 cups hot water

Whirl all the ingredients in a blender at high speed until liquefied.
Strain in a sieve, pressing out the liquid. The milk can by used in
recipes and freezes well. (Use the coconut left in the sieve for baking.)
Makes 2 cups.

* Suitable for the Elimination Diet

⋖§§⋗ BANANA SHAKE*

2 cups water
⅓ cup raw cashews (optional)
1 or 2 large frozen bananas, cut into pieces
1 tablespoon honey
½ teaspoon vanilla
2 tablespoons soy powder (optional)

Pour the water into the container of a blender. If using cashews, add
them and process on high to make a nut milk. Add the bananas a
few pieces at a time and blend until smooth. Add the other ingredients
and blend to mix thoroughly. Serve immediately.

Hint: To freeze the bananas, peel and wrap in plastic wrap and
freeze until solid.

Makes 3 cups.

Variations, if Tolerated:
– Substitute an equal amount of milk for the milk substitute.
– Substitute an equal amount of sugar for the honey.
– Add 2 fresh ripe peaches in addition to the bananas.

* Suitable for the Elimination Diet

❧ SOYA SHAKE*

    1 cup water
    1 tablespoon soya powder
    2 tablespoons carob powder (optional)
    1 cup soy milk
    ½ cup cracked ice
    1 sliced banana
    1 teaspoon honey
    ⅛ teaspoon vanilla

Pour the water into the container of a blender and add the soya and carob powders. Blend on high speed until well combined. Add the soy milk, ice, sliced banana, honey, and vanilla and blend thoroughly.

Note: Berries, cherries, peaches, and other allowed fruit may be used in place of the banana.

Makes 2½ cups.

* **Suitable for the Elimination Diet**

❧ TROPICAL SHAKE*

    1 frozen banana
    ½ cup flaked, unsweetened coconut
    2 tablespoons peanut butter or nut butter
    2½ cups nut milk or other milk substitute
    ½ teaspoon pure vanilla

Puree the banana, coconut, peanut butter, and 1 cup of the nut milk or allowed substitute. Blend until creamy, then add the remaining nut milk and vanilla.

Makes 4 cups.

   Variations, if Tolerated:
− Substitute an equal amount of milk for the milk substitute.

* **Suitable for the Elimination Diet**

❧ FRESH MELON SHAKE*

½ cup pineapple juice
2 cups sliced or cubed ripe melon

Pour the juice into the container of a blender and, at high speed, add the sliced fruit a few pieces at a time. Blend thoroughly, adding more cantaloupe if a thicker shake is desired.

Makes 2½ cups.

* Suitable for the Elimination Diet

❧ BANANA PINEAPPLE COOLER*

2 cups cold pineapple juice
5 to 6 pineapple chunks
2 ripe bananas, cut into pieces

Pour the pineapple juice into the container of a blender and, at high speed, add the chunks of fruit a few at a time. Blend until smooth and frothy.

Makes 3 cups.

* Suitable for the Elimination Diet

❧ APRICOT-APPLE SHAKE*

1 16-ounce can water-pack apricots, drained
½ cup applesauce
½ cup nut milk, soy milk, or goat's milk
6 to 10 ice cubes

Combine all the ingredients in a blender and liquefy.

Makes 2¾ cups.

Variations, if Tolerated:
– Substitute an equal amount of milk for the milk substitute.

* **Suitable for the Elimination Diet**

❦❧ FRUIT SLUSH*

> 2 cups water
> ½ cup fresh pineapple chunks
> ½ cup frozen strawberries
> Sweetener to taste

Blend the ingredients together until mixed well. Serve immediately.

Hint: To prepare frozen strawberries, wash the strawberries and remove their stems. Arrange the strawberries on a cookie sheet and place in the freezer. Freeze until solid (1 to 2 hours). If not using the strawberries right away, put them in a freezer container.

Makes 3 cups.

Variations, if Tolerated:
– Substitute an equal amount of milk for the water.

* **Suitable for the Elimination Diet**

❦❧ KIWIFRUIT SPRITZER†

> 3 kiwifruit, peeled
> 2 tablespoons sugar or other sweetener
> ½ cup orange juice
> 1½ cups club soda

Combine the kiwifruit, sugar, and orange juice in a blender. Whirl until smooth. Pour ½ cup into a tall (12-ounce) glass. Add ice and pour in ½ cup club soda. Stir to combine. Garnish with kiwifruit slices, lemon wedges, or mint. Serve immediately.

Makes 3 spritzers.

† **Free of milk, egg, wheat, corn**

RECIPES

❦ BANANA PEACH DRINK†

2 very ripe bananas, cut into pieces
2 very ripe peaches, peeled and sliced
1 cup goat's milk or milk substitute
¼ cup sugar
2 teaspoons lemon juice
Mint leaves

Freeze banana slices and peaches until very firm. When fruits are frozen, place in a blender with the milk, sugar, and lemon juice. Blend at high speed, pushing the fruit down carefully, until the mixture is blended and has the consistency of soft ice cream. Garnish with fresh mint leaves and fruit slices, if desired. Serve immediately.

Makes 2 cups.

† **Free of milk, egg, wheat, corn**

9 · BREADS, MUFFINS, BISCUITS, AND CRACKERS

For the person who has food allergies, especially to milk, eggs, and wheat, finding acceptable breads can be a major problem.

In our kitchen we experimented with many different ingredients. Our first batch of milk-, egg-, and wheat-free muffins turned out so rubbery that they could bounce. Of course, that was the day that a newspaper reporter came out to write a story about our research kitchen! It made the front pages.

Try these recipes first, and once you have gained some experience in allergy-free cooking, create your own favorites. Don't be afraid to use new ingredients such as oats, amaranth, xanthan gum, tapioca starch, or buckwheat.

QUICK BREADS

✦§§✦ OATMEAL BREAD*

This delicious bread is great for making sandwiches.

> 1 cup rolled oats
> 1 cup hot water
> ½ cup maple syrup or honey
> ¼ teaspoon sea salt
> 1 mashed banana
> 1 cup oat flour
> ¼ teaspoon baking soda
> 3 teaspoons baking powder

Preheat the oven to 350°F. Grease a 9-by-5-inch loaf pan.

Mix the rolled oats with the hot water. Let stand for 5 minutes. Stir in the honey, salt, and banana. Add the flour, baking soda, and baking powder and stir until all the ingredients are just mixed. Do not overmix. Turn into the loaf pan and let stand for 20 minutes in a warm place. Bake for 45 minutes.

Makes 1 loaf.

Variations, if Tolerated:
– Substitute an equal amount of sugar for the honey.
– Add 2 eggs in place of or in addition to the mashed banana.
– Add ½ cup chopped nuts or raisins.

* **Suitable for the Elimination Diet**

❧❦ CARROT BREAD*

1 cup shredded raw carrots
¾ cup maple syrup or maple sugar
¾ cup safflower oil
1½ cups oat flour
1 teaspoon baking soda
2 teaspoons baking powder
1 teaspoon cinnamon (optional)
½ teaspoon sea salt
½ cup raisins
¼ cup chopped walnuts

Preheat the oven to 350°F. Grease the bottom of a 9-by-5-inch or 8-by-4-inch loaf pan.

In a large bowl, combine the carrots, syrup, and oil. Stir for 1 minute. Add the flour, cinnamon, baking soda, baking powder, and sea salt. Stir until just combined. Mix in the raisins and nuts and pour into the loaf pan. Bake for 1 hour, or until a tester inserted in the center comes out clean. Remove from the pan and cool completely.

Makes 1 loaf.

Variations, if Tolerated:
– Add 1 egg along with the syrup and oil.
– Substitute 2 cups of wheat for the oat flour.

* Suitable for the Elimination Diet

✦◦§◦✦ APRICOT ALMOND BREAD†

1¾ cups dried unsulfured apricots
¼ cup allowed margarine
1½ cups sugar
2 cups wheat flour
2 teaspoons baking powder
½ teaspoon baking soda
½ teaspoon salt
⅓ cup coconut milk or water
½ cup chopped almonds

Preheat the oven to 350°F. Grease a 9-by-5-inch loaf pan.

In a small saucepan, add enough water to cover the apricots and simmer for 5 minutes. Drain the fruit and reserve the juice. Chop the apricots. Cream the margarine and sugar and stir in ½ cup of the reserved apricot juice. Combine the flour with the baking powder, baking soda, and salt. Stir the dry ingredients into the creamed mixture alternately with coconut milk, stirring the batter only until combined. Fold in the almonds. Pour the batter into the loaf pan and bake for 1 hour, or until done.

Makes 1 loaf.

Variations, if Tolerated:

− Substitute an equal amount of milk for the coconut milk or water.

† **Free of milk, egg, corn, citrus**

✒️ ZUCCHINI NUT BREAD†

    3 eggs
    ¾ cup oil
    1 cup honey
    2 cups grated and tightly packed zucchini
    3 cups barley flour
    2 teaspoons baking powder
    ½ teaspoon baking soda
    ½ teaspoon salt
    1½ teaspoons cinnamon (optional)
    ½ teaspoon ground ginger
    1½ teaspoons vanilla
    1 cup chopped nuts

Preheat the oven to 350°F. Grease three 7½-by-3½-inch or two 9-by-5-inch loaf pans and dust with barley flour. Shake out the excess flour.

Beat the eggs in a large mixing bowl. Stir in the oil and honey, then the zucchini. Combine the dry ingredients and add to the bowl. Gently stir in the vanilla and nuts. Pour the batter into loaf pans. Bake for 50 to 55 minutes, or until done. Let stand a few minutes, then turn onto a wire rack to cool. Wrapped tightly, the bread freezes well.

Makes 2 or 3 loaves.

Variations, if Tolerated:
− Substitute an equal amount of sugar for the honey.
− Substitute 3 cups of wheat flour for the barley flour.

† **Free of milk, wheat, sugar, corn, citrus**

❧❦❧ BANANA BREAD†

    ⅔ cup oil
    1 cup sugar
    2 eggs
    1½ cups mashed ripe bananas
    1 tablespoon lemon juice
    1¾ cups wheat flour
    1 teaspoon salt
    1 teaspoon baking soda

Preheat the oven to 325°F. Grease a 9-by-5-inch or 8½-by-4½-inch (for a taller loaf) loaf pan.

In a large bowl, mix the oil and sugar. Add the eggs one at a time, beating well after each addition. Blend in the bananas and lemon juice. Mix together the flour, salt, and baking soda and stir into the banana mixture. Pour into a loaf pan and bake for 1 hour 10 minutes, or until done. Remove from the pan and cool on a wire rack.

Makes 1 loaf.

† **Free of milk, corn**

❦ STREUSEL-TOPPED COFFEE CAKE†

2 cups oat flour
⅓ cup sugar
1 tablespoon baking powder
½ teaspoon salt
¼ cup soft margarine or butter
2 eggs
½ to ⅔ cup milk, nut milk, soy milk, or goat's milk

Topping

¼ cup packed brown sugar OR ⅛ cup honey or maple
   syrup
1 teaspoon cinnamon (optional)
¼ cup chopped nuts
1 tablespoon margarine or butter, melted

Preheat the oven to 375°F. Lightly grease an 8-inch square pan.

Mix together the oat flour, sugar, baking powder, and salt. Add the margarine, sweetener, eggs, and milk. Beat until smooth. Pour the batter into the pan. Mix the topping ingredients together and sprinkle onto the batter. Bake for 30 to 35 minutes.

† **Free of wheat, corn, citrus**

YEAST BREADS

◆§§◆ RICE-FLOUR BREAD†

> 2¼ cups warm water
> 4½ teaspoons dry yeast
> ¼ cup honey
> 4¼ cups brown rice flour
> ½ cup ground sunflower seeds
> 1 carrot, grated
> 4½ teaspoons xanthan gum
> 1 teaspoon cinnamon
> 1 teaspoon wheat-free tamari, dried herbs, or grated
>   lemon rind
> ⅓ cup oil
> 2 eggs (optional)
> 2 to 4 tablespoons sesame seeds

Preheat the oven to 200°F. Grease two 8-by-4-inch loaf pans.

Combine the water, yeast, and honey in a cup. Set aside for 10 minutes, until the yeast is foamy. Place the flour in a large bowl in a 200°F. oven for 10 to 15 minutes to warm it. (Then preheat the oven to 400°F.) Remove 1 cup of the flour and reserve. To the remaining flour add the sunflower seeds, carrot, xanthan gum, cinnamon, and tamari. Mix well.

Make a well in the center of the flour and add the oil, eggs, and the yeast mixture. Using an electric mixer, beat at high speed for 3 minutes. Stop and scrape the sides of the bowl. Add the reserved flour. Beat at low speed for 1 minute. Scrape the batter off the beaters and level the surface of the dough. Oil the top of the dough and the sides of the bowl above the dough. Cover the bowl with a damp towel. Place in a draft-free place to rise. Allow to rise for 1½ to 2½ hours, until doubled in bulk. Do not rush this step. Yeast should work slowly.

To knead the dough, beat with an electric mixer for 3 minutes. Scatter sesame seeds in bottoms of the loaf pans, especially in corners. Divide the dough between the pans, pushing it into the corners with a spatula and smoothing the tops. Sprinkle with sesame seeds. Allow to rise, uncovered, for 30 to 35 minutes, until the dough just reaches the tops of the pans. Don't let it go higher or it may collapse. Bake at 400°F for 10 minutes. Place foil loosely over the loaves and bake 50 minutes more.

Note: The secret to making yeast-raised gluten-free bread is the xanthan gum. See the appendix for purchasing sources.

Makes 2 loaves.

† **Free of milk, wheat, sugar, corn**

✍§ε PUMPERNICKEL BREAD†

Of German origin, this recipe makes a firm black bread. Because rye has little gluten, it will not rise as much as bread made from wheat flour.

> 6 cups rye flour
> 1 tablespoon salt
> ¼ cup margarine
> 2 tablespoons molasses or honey
> 1¼ cups milk, nut milk, soy milk, or goat's milk
> 1 package dry yeast
> ⅔ cup tepid water
> 1 tablespoon caraway seeds

Preheat the oven to 400°F. Lightly grease two 9-by-5-inch loaf pans or a cookie sheet.

In a large bowl, mix the rye flour and salt. Cut the margarine into small pieces and cut into the flour. In a small saucepan, combine the molasses and milk. Cook over very low heat until the molasses has dissolved and the milk is lukewarm. Combine the yeast and water and mix until the yeast is dissolved. Make a well in the flour mixture and pour in the yeast liquid and the warm milk and molasses. Mix until a sticky dough has formed.

Turn the dough out onto a floured surface and knead it well for 10 minutes, or until the dough is firm and no longer sticky. Add more flour if necessary. Put the dough into a lightly greased bowl and cover with greased plastic wrap, or put it into a large greased plastic bag. Allow the dough to rise in a warm place for 45 to 60 minutes, or until it has doubled in bulk.

When the dough has risen, turn it out onto a lightly floured surface and knead it again for 2 to 3 minutes. Divide the dough in half, shape it into two ovals, and put them on a lightly greased baking sheet or into two loaf pans. Sprinkle caraway seeds over the loaves and press the seeds into the dough. Cover the dough and put in a warm place to rise until doubled in bulk or risen to the top of the pans. Bake for 45 minutes, or until the loaves are dark brown and sound hollow when tapped underneath. Cool on a wire rack.

Makes 2 loaves.

† **Free of egg, wheat, sugar, corn, citrus**

MUFFINS

✿❀❀ PEANUT BUTTER RICE MUFFINS*

> 1 cup rice flour
> 4 teaspoons baking powder
> ¼ teaspoon sea salt
> 2 tablespoons maple sugar
> 1 tablespoon safflower oil
> ½ cup nut milk or water
> 1 tablespoon peanut butter

Preheat the oven to 425°F. Grease a 6-cup muffin tin.

Mix the dry ingredients together. Add the oil, nut milk, and peanut butter and mix. Fill the muffin cups two-thirds full. Bake for about 20 minutes.

Makes 6 muffins.

Variations, if Tolerated:
— Substitute an equal amount of sugar for the maple sugar.
— Substitute an equal amount of milk for the nut milk or water.
— Substitute 1¼ cups of wheat flour for the rice flour.
— Add 1 egg with the oil and liquid and decrease the baking powder to 2 teaspoons.

* **Suitable for the Elimination Diet**

❧ RICE-FLOUR MUFFINS*

> ½ cup pureed banana or strawberries
> ½ cup nut milk or water
> 1 cup rice flour
> ¼ teaspoon sea salt
> 1½ teaspoons baking powder
> 1 tablespoon milk-free, corn-free margarine, melted

Preheat the oven to 350°F. Grease a 6-cup muffin tin.

Stir the fruit pulp into the nut milk. Add the dry ingredients and margarine. Mix until moistened. Fill the muffin cups two-thirds full. Bake for 15 to 20 minutes.

Makes 6 muffins.

Variations, if Tolerated:

– Substitute an equal amount of milk in place of the nut milk or water.
– Add 1 egg to the liquid and decrease the baking powder to 1 teaspoon.

* **Suitable for the Elimination Diet**

❧ SOYA POTATO MUFFINS*

> 1 cup soy flour
> 1 cup potato starch
> 1 teaspoon salt
> 2 tablespoons baking powder
> 2 tablespoons maple sugar
> ½ cup milk-free, corn-free margarine, melted
> ¾ to 1 cup soy milk or water

Preheat the oven to 350°F. Grease a 12-muffin tin.

Sift the dry ingredients together three times. Add the margarine and soy milk. Beat well. Fill the muffin cups two-thirds full. Bake for 25 to 30 minutes.

Makes 12 muffins.

Variations, if Tolerated:
- Substitute an equal amount of sugar for the maple sugar.
- Substitute an equal amount of milk for the soy milk or water.
- Add 1 egg to the liquid and decrease the baking powder to 2 teaspoons.

* **Suitable for the Elimination Diet**

⤐⧽⤖ SOYA MUFFINS*

⅓ cup soy flour
⅓ cup rice flour
⅓ cup potato starch or tapioca starch
½ teaspoon sea salt
4 tablespoons maple sugar
3 teaspoons baking powder
½ cup riced boiled potatoes
½ cup soy milk or water
2 tablespoons safflower oil

Preheat the oven to 400°F. Grease a 6-cup muffin tin.

Mix the dry ingredients together. Mix the potatoes, soy milk, and oil in a separate bowl. Combine all the ingredients. Do not beat. Fill the muffin cups two-thirds full. Bake for 25 to 30 minutes. Remove from the pan immediately and allow the muffins to cool on a wire rack.

Makes 6 muffins.

Variations, if Tolerated:
- Substitute an equal amount of sugar for the maple sugar.
- Substitute an equal amount of milk for the soy milk or water.
- Add 1 egg to the liquid and decrease the baking powder to 2 teaspoons.

* **Suitable for the Elimination Diet**

❧ CORN MUFFINS†

> ¾ cup rice flour
> 1 cup cornmeal
> 1½ tablespoons baking powder
> ½ teaspoon salt
> ¼ cup sugar
> 1 egg, slightly beaten
> ¼ cup milk-free margarine, melted
> 1 cup water

Preheat the oven to 425°F. Grease a 12-cup muffin tin.

In a medium-size bowl, stir together the rice flour, cornmeal, baking powder, salt, and sugar. Add the margarine, egg, and water to the dry ingredients and stir until smooth. Pour the batter into muffin cups. Bake for 25 minutes, or until the muffins pull away from the sides of the cups. Remove the muffins from the tin.

Makes 12 muffins.

Variations, if Tolerated:
– Substitute an equal amount of milk for the water.

† **Free of milk, wheat, citrus**

❧❦❧ OAT MUFFINS†

    1 cup sifted oat flour
    3½ teaspoons baking powder
    1½ teaspoons sugar
    ⅛ teaspoon salt
    ¼ cup cold water or oat milk
    2 tablespoons allowed margarine, melted

Preheat the oven to 425°F. Grease a 6- or 8-cup muffin tin.

Sift the dry ingredients into a medium-size bowl. Add the liquid and mix until smooth. Stir in the margarine. Pour into muffin tins and bake for 25 minutes.

Makes 6 to 8 muffins.

CINNAMON RAISIN MUFFINS

Add ½ teaspoon cinnamon and ½ cup raisins to the dry ingredients.

NUT MUFFINS

Add ½ cup chopped nuts to the dry ingredients.

BANANA OAT MUFFINS

Add ½ cup mashed ripe banana after the other ingredients are mixed. You may reduce the oat flour to ¾ cup and add ¼ cup quick oats.

Variations, if Tolerated:
– Substitute an equal amount of milk for the water or oat milk.
– Add 1 egg to the liquid and decrease the baking powder to 2 teaspoons.

† **Free of milk, egg, wheat, corn, citrus**

BISCUITS AND CRACKERS

✺ RICE BAKING-POWDER BISCUITS*

> ⅝ cup rice flour
> 3 teaspoons baking powder
> ⅛ teaspoon salt
> ½ teaspoon maple sugar
> ¼ cup soybean shortening
> ¼ cup soy milk

Preheat the oven to 350°F.

Mix the dry ingredients together. Cut in the shortening, then stir in the soy milk. Lightly knead the dough on a board lightly floured with rice flour. Roll out to about ½ inch thick and cut with a 2-inch cookie cutter or glass. Place on an ungreased baking sheet 2 inches apart. Bake for 10 minutes.

Makes 6 to 8 biscuits.

Variations, if Tolerated:
– Substitute an equal amount of sugar for the maple sugar.
– Substitute an equal amount of milk for the soy milk.

* Suitable for the Elimination Diet

✺ SCOTTISH OATCAKES*

These oatcakes may be served warm or cold, with butter or jam.

> ⅔ cup oatmeal
> ⅛ teaspoon salt
> ¼ teaspoon baking soda
> ½ teaspoon cinnamon (optional)
> 2 tablespoons allowed margarine
> 1 tablespoon water

Preheat the oven to 400°F. Grease a cookie sheet.

In a medium-size bowl, mix together the oats, salt, baking soda, and cinnamon. In a small saucepan, slowly heat the margarine and water until the margarine has melted. Bring to a boil, then pour into the oatmeal mixture. Stir to form a soft dough. Mix the dough together with your hands, then turn it onto a floured surface and knead lightly. Roll the dough out thinly to form a circle 8 inches in diameter. Cut the round into 8 wedges. Using a spatula, carefully lift the wedges onto a cookie sheet. Bake for 15 to 20 minutes, or until the oatcakes are crisp, lightly brown, and the edges begin to curl up.

Makes 8 wedges.

* **Suitable for the Elimination Diet**

❧ OATMEAL CRACKERS*

> 1 cup water
> ½ cup cooking oil
> 1 teaspoon sea salt
> 4 cups oat flour

Preheat the oven to 350°F. Grease a cookie sheet.

Combine all the ingredients until a stiff dough is formed. Chill. Lightly flour a board and roll out the dough to ⅛ inch thick. Transfer the dough to the cookie sheet. Cut into squares and prick with a fork. Bake for about 20 minutes.

Makes approximately 48 crackers.

* **Suitable for the Elimination Diet**

⤐❦❧ RYE CRISPS*

This wafer-thin crisp bread can be eaten as a cracker or as a substitute for bread.

> 2 cups rye flour
> 1/2 teaspoon salt
> 1/4 cup allowed margarine
> 1/4 cup water

Preheat the oven to 400°F. Lightly grease two baking sheets.

In a mixing bowl, combine the rye flour and salt. Cut in the margarine. Stir in the water and mix until the ingredients are thoroughly blended and the dough is firm. Divide the dough in half. Knead each piece lightly on a floured surface. Roll out thinly to about 9 inches square. Cut into 3-inch squares and put the squares on the baking sheets. Prick each square well with a fork to keep it from rising and bubbling. Bake the rye crisps for 10 to 15 minutes, or until the edges just begin to color, but do not let them brown. Cool slightly on the baking sheets, then transfer the crackers to wire racks.

Makes 18 rye crisps.

Variations, if Tolerated:
– Add 1 teaspoon dried mixed herbs to the dry ingredients.

* Suitable for the Elimination Diet

10 · CEREALS AND PANCAKES

Breakfast doesn't have to be the most difficult meal of the day. Since most people are in a hurry at breakfast time, you'll need to plan ahead and prepare part of the meal ahead of time.

In this chapter you'll find recipes for cereals and pancakes. Try the Apple Cinnamon Crunchy Granola; it's great as a snack too. For other breakfast ideas, see Chapter 9 on breads, muffins, crackers, and biscuits. Some puddings can make great morning treats, such as Rice Pudding (recipe, page 166). On days when you are running late, try making a "blender breakfast." Look at Chapter 8 for some quick beverage ideas.

Finally, don't limit your breakfast to typical morning meals; warm up tasty leftovers or have some steaming hot homemade soup.

❧❧❧ APPLE OATMEAL*

    1 cup rolled oats
    2 cups cold water
    ½ teaspoon sea salt
    2 apples, peeled, cored, and chopped
    Dash of nutmeg

Combine the oats, water, and salt in a saucepan. Cook for 10 minutes over low heat. Add the apples and nutmeg. Cook 5 minutes more, or until the apples are done to the desired consistency. Serve with nut milk and honey.

Makes 4 servings.

Variations:
– Use raisins or dates in place of the apples.

* Suitable for the Elimination Diet

❧❧❧ GRANOLA*

    ¼ cup unsweetened applesauce
    ¼ to ½ cup honey
    1 tablespoon oil
    1 tablespoon vanilla
    ¾ teaspoon sea salt
    2¼ cups rolled oats
    ½ cup sliced almonds or cashews
    ¼ cup grated coconut
    ¼ cup raisins (optional)

Preheat the oven to 375°F.

Mix the applesauce, honey, oil, vanilla, and salt in large bowl. Add the oats, nuts, and coconut. Stir just long enough to coat the dry ingredients. Spread in a 13-by-9-inch pan and bake for 20 to 25 minutes, stirring occasionally. Cool and add the raisins, if desired. Store in an airtight container. Eat within 2 weeks.

Makes 4 cups.

* Suitable for the Elimination Diet

✨ APPLE CINNAMON CRUNCHY GRANOLA*

4 cups rolled oats
½ cup grated or flaked coconut
1 cup finely chopped nuts
½ cup raw sesame seeds
¾ teaspoon sea salt
1 teaspoon cinnamon
½ cup honey
⅓ cup safflower oil
½ teaspoon vanilla
8 ounces unsulfured dried apples, finely chopped

Preheat the oven to 350°F. Grease two large cookie sheets.

Combine the oats, coconut, nuts, sesame seeds, salt, and cinnamon in a large bowl. In small saucepan, combine the honey, oil, and vanilla and heat gently to liquefy the honey. Add to the oat mixture and mix thoroughly. Spread on the cookie sheets and bake for 20 to 25 minutes, stirring occasionally. Add the apples. Store in a tightly covered container in the refrigerator.

Makes 8 servings.

* Suitable for the Elimination Diet

⮡§⭒ **PANCAKE OR WAFFLE BATTER***

> 1 cup oat flour
> 2 teaspoons baking powder
> 2 tablespoons safflower oil
> ¾ cup pineapple juice or water
> 1 tablespoon maple syrup or maple sugar

Mix the flour and baking powder together. In a separate bowl, combine the juice and maple syrup and stir lightly. Add to the dry ingredients and stir until well mixed.

Makes 9 pancakes or 4 waffles.

Variations, if Tolerated:
– Substitute an equal amount of milk for the pineapple juice or water.
– Substitute an equal amount of sugar for the maple sugar.
– Substitute ⅞ cup wheat flour for the oat flour.
– Add 1 egg to the liquids and decrease the baking powder to 1 teaspoon.

* Suitable for the Elimination Diet

❧ RICE WAFFLES*

2 cups rice flour
4 teaspoons baking powder
1 tablespoon maple sugar
2 cups nut milk or goat's milk
3 tablespoons safflower oil

Sift the dry ingredients together. Add the nut milk and oil gradually, stirring the mixture constantly until smooth. Bake in a hot waffle iron.

Makes 4 to 6 waffles.

Variations, if Tolerated:
— Substitute an equal amount of milk for the nut or goat's milk.
— Substitute an equal amount of sugar for the maple sugar.
— Substitute 2¼ cups wheat flour for the rice flour.
— Add 1 egg to the liquids and decrease the baking powder to 2 teaspoons.

* Suitable for the Elimination Diet

RECIPES

❧❧ POTATO PANCAKES*

1 cup mashed potatoes, seasoned
1 cup finely grated uncooked potatoes
2 tablespoons milk-free, corn-free margarine
½ teaspoon sea salt
½ teaspoon baking powder

Combine all the ingredients and shape into pancakes. A little oat flour may be added, if necessary, to hold the cakes together. Sprinkle both sides of the cakes with oat flour. Heat oil over medium heat. Place the pancakes in the oil and allow the raw potatoes to cook. Serve with maple syrup.

Makes 4 servings.

* Suitable for the Elimination Diet

❧❧ DUTCH POTATO PANCAKES*

4 or 5 large potatoes
¼ cup oat flour
¼ teaspoon sea salt
¼ cup coconut milk, nut milk, or goat's milk

Peel the potatoes (if desired) and grate. Make a paste of flour, salt, and coconut milk. Add to the grated potatoes. Drop into a hot greased pan and fry approximately 5 minutes on each side, until browned and cooked throughout. Serve with allowed margarine and maple syrup.

Makes 4 servings.

Variations, if Tolerated:
— Try an equal amount of brown rice flour or wheat flour. Do not use potato starch or tapioca starch as a flour substitute.
— Substitute an equal amount of milk for the coconut milk, nut milk, or goat's milk.

* Suitable for the Elimination Diet

11 · SALADS AND SALAD DRESSINGS

I love fresh, crisp, green salads with my homemade French Dressing. It certainly beats any bottled salad dressings. I also love making exotic and unusual salads. I try to create new salads by adding fruits, like sliced kiwi, or vegetables, nuts, seeds, or meats. Sometimes I make a whole meal out of a salad, and serve a variety of homemade breads.

When there is such a variety of ingredients available, you don't feel as though you're making "allergy-free" foods. You're just having fun cooking.

SALADS

⋙⋘ SALMON SALAD*

2 cups drained canned salmon (packed in water)
¼ cup diced onion
1 cup diced celery
1 cup homemade mayonnaise (recipe, p. 172)
½ teaspoon salt
Pepper to taste

Mix all the ingredients together and store in the refrigerator. Serve over lettuce or on sandwiches.

Makes 3 cups.

* **Suitable for the Elimination Diet**

RECIPES

❧ AVOCADO STUFFED WITH TUNA*

2 ripe avocados
1 7-ounce can water-packed solid white tuna, drained
1 cup chopped walnuts
1 cup homemade mayonnaise (recipe, p. 172)
1½ tablespoons tomato paste
Salt and pepper

Halve and pit the avocados. Scoop out the flesh without tearing the shells. Dice the flesh into ¾-inch pieces. In a bowl, mix the drained tuna chunks, ⅔ cup walnuts, mayonnaise, and tomato paste. Add the avocado. Season with salt and pepper and toss lightly. Divide the salad among the avocado shells and garnish with the remaining walnuts.

Makes 4 servings.

* Suitable for the Elimination Diet

❧ TUNA SALAD LUAU*

¾ cup homemade mayonnaise (recipe, p. 172)
¾ teaspoon curry powder
2 6½-ounce cans water-packed flaked tuna, drained
1 20-ounce can pineapple chunks, drained
1 cup sliced celery
½ cup chopped walnuts
1 tablespoon chopped fresh parsley
Sea salt and pepper to taste
Lettuce leaves

Mix the mayonnaise with the curry powder. Combine the remaining ingredients except the seasonings and lettuce leaves. Add the mayonnaise mixture and season to taste. Toss lightly. Chill until ready to serve. Serve on lettuce.

Makes 4 to 6 servings.

* Suitable for the Elimination Diet

CRABMEAT SALAD*

> 1 pound fresh crabmeat
> ½ medium onion, finely chopped
> Salt and pepper to taste
> ½ cup allowed oil
> ½ cup vinegar
> ½ cup ice water

Remove any bits of shell and cartilage from the crabmeat. Place half of the chopped onion in the bottom of a bowl. Arrange the crabmeat on top of the onion. Spread the remaining onion over the crab. Salt and pepper to taste. Pour oil, then vinegar, and finally ice water over the crab mixture. Cover and refrigerate for 2 to 12 hours. Toss lightly just before serving.

Makes 4 servings.

* **Suitable for the Elimination Diet**

SUNFLOWER SALAD*

> 2 cups coarsely shredded carrots
> 1 cup thinly sliced celery
> 2 firm bananas, sliced
> ½ cup sunflower seeds
> ¼ cup sunflower or safflower oil
> 2 tablespoons unsweetened pineapple juice
> ¼ teaspoon sea salt
> ¼ teaspoon pepper
> Crisp lettuce cups

Combine the carrots, celery, bananas, and sunflower seeds. Stir the oil, juice, salt, and pepper together. Pour over the salad mixture and toss lightly. Serve in lettuce cups.

Makes 4 servings.

* **Suitable for the Elimination Diet**

ເ♥ POTATO SALAD*

6 cups cooked, peeled, and cubed potatoes (6 medium)
¼ cup chopped onion
¾ cup chopped celery (1 large stalk)
1½ cups sliced fresh mushrooms
⅓ cup homemade mayonnaise (recipe, p. 172)
1 teaspoon sea salt
¼ teaspoon pepper
¼ cup sunflower seeds

In a large bowl, combine all the ingredients except the sunflower seeds. Toss gently until well mixed. Refrigerate. Just before serving, toss with the sunflower seeds.

Makes 6 servings.

* **Suitable for the Elimination Diet**

✌⧵⧸➤ BANANA HONEY SALAD*

> Lettuce leaves
> 1 banana
> ¼ cup peanut butter
> ¼ cup honey
> 1 tablespoon shredded coconut
> 2 teaspoons pineapple juice

Arrange lettuce leaves on two salad plates. Slice the banana in half, then slice lengthwise. Place the banana slices on top of the lettuce leaves. Sprinkle with pineapple juice to keep them from turning dark. Mix the peanut butter and honey. Spoon over the banana slices and sprinkle with coconut.

Makes 2 servings.

* Suitable for the Elimination Diet

✌⧵⧸➤ MOLDED FRUIT GELATIN*

> 1 envelope unflavored gelatin
> ¼ cup cold water
> 1 cup hot water
> ½ cup unsweetened pineapple, grape, or apple juice
> Sweetener to taste
> Pinch of sea salt
> 1 cup fruit (optional)

Soften the gelatin in the cold water. Add the hot water and stir until dissolved. Add the juice, sweetener, and salt. Pour into a mold and add the fruit after the gelatin has thickened slightly. Chill until firm. Serve in lettuce cups, if desired.

Makes 4 servings.

Variations, if Tolerated:
– Add 2 cups diced tart apples, ½ cup chopped pecans, and ½ cup diced celery to the gelatin mixture and pour into the mold.

* Suitable for the Elimination Diet

❧§❧ SUNNY SALAD†

>2 tablespoons orange juice
>2 tablespoons lemon juice
>½ teaspoon salt
>2 teaspoons sweetener
>1 cup grated carrots
>1 cup grated cabbage
>1 cup chopped, unpeeled apples

Combine the orange juice, lemon juice, salt, and sweetener. Mix the carrots, cabbage, and apples together. Pour the juices over the salad and toss.

Makes 6 servings.

† **Free of milk, egg, wheat, corn**

❧§❧ ORANGE RICE SALAD†

>3 tablespoons wine vinegar
>5 tablespoons allowed oil, such as safflower oil
>3 tablespoons orange juice
>1 tablespoon chopped fresh parsley
>4 cups warm cooked rice
>2 oranges or 2 cans mandarin oranges, well drained
>1 celery stalk, thinly sliced
>½ cup seedless raisins
>½ cup chopped walnuts

Pour the wine vinegar into a small bowl and add the oil, 1 tablespoon at a time, beating vigorously with a fork after each addition. Add the orange juice and parsley and beat again. Put the warm cooked rice into a large mixing bowl. Add ⅓ cup of the dressing and mix thoroughly. The warm rice will absorb the dressing. Peel and remove the pith from the oranges. Cut away the membrane from the segments of fruit. Add the orange segments or mandarin oranges to the rice along with the celery, raisins, and nuts. Mix well. Chill before serving. This salad will keep well in the refrigerator for up to 2 days; add more dressing before serving.

Makes 4 to 6 servings.

† Free of milk, egg, wheat, corn, sugar

❧§ APPLE GELATIN SALAD†

    4 cups unsweetened apple juice
    3 tablespoons sweetener
    ¼ teaspoon salt
    2 envelopes unflavored gelatin
    5 red eating apples (unpeeled) or enough to make 3 cups
       shredded
    4 tablespoons lemon juice
    1 teaspoon grated lemon rind
    ½ cup finely chopped celery
    1 cup chopped walnuts
    Salad greens for garnish

In a medium-size saucepan, combine the apple juice, sweetener, salt, and gelatin. Stir until blended. Heat and stir until the gelatin is dissolved. Remove from the heat and allow to cool. Refrigerate for about 2 hours, until the mixture thickens to the consistency of unbeaten egg whites. Wash the apples. Core and slice one apple, sprinkle with 1 tablespoon lemon juice, and reserve for garnish. Core and shred the remaining apples. Stir in the rest of the lemon juice to keep the apples from turning dark. Sprinkle the lemon rind over the apples. Add the celery and nuts and stir into the thickened gelatin. Turn the mixture into a 6-cup mold and refrigerate for 4 to 6 hours, until set. Unmold and serve; garnish with salad greens and the reserved apple slices.

Makes 10 to 12 servings.

† Free of milk, egg, wheat, corn

&§& CHICKEN RICE SALAD WITH CASHEWS†

    3 cups diced cooked chicken
    2 green onions, sliced thin
    ½ cup diced celery
    3 cups cooked rice
    1 cup allowed mayonnaise
    1 tablespoon lemon juice
    1 teaspoon allowed sweetener
    1 teaspoon salt
    ½ cup cashews, raw or roasted
    Salad greens for garnish

Combine the chicken, onions, celery, and rice in a large bowl. In a small bowl, combine the mayonnaise, lemon juice, sweetener, and salt; mix well. Pour the dressing over the chicken mixture and toss lightly but thoroughly. Adjust the seasonings; mix lightly. Refrigerate, covered, for about 2 hours before serving to blend the flavors. Just before serving, add the cashews and mix lightly. Serve on crisp salad greens.

Makes 6 servings.

† **Free of milk, egg, wheat, corn**

SALAD DRESSINGS

✚❀❧ FRENCH DRESSING*

> ½ cup safflower oil
> ⅓ cup apple cider vinegar
> ⅓ cup homemade catsup (recipe, p. 171) OR
>   2 tablespoons tomato paste
> ¼ cup honey
> 1 teaspoon paprika
> ½ teaspoon sea salt
> ½ medium onion, grated (optional)

Mix together and shake well before pouring on salad.

✚❀❧ PINEAPPLE HONEY DRESSING*

> ½ cup honey
> ¼ cup pineapple juice
> ¼ teaspoon sea salt
> 3 tablespoons crushed pineapple

Mix well and serve over fruit salad or greens.

* Suitable for the Elimination Diet

❧ HONEY APPLE DRESSING*

> 2 tablespoons honey
> ¼ cup apple juice
> ½ cup safflower oil

Mix the ingredients together well. Season to taste with sea salt, pepper, and herbs as desired.

* Suitable for the Elimination Diet

12 · SOUPS AND STEWS

Thank goodness for the invention of electric slow cookers. After dinner, whenever there are extra chicken, turkey or beef bones, we put them into the pot, add some water, an onion, and some celery leaves, let them simmer for a few hours, and then chill overnight. The next morning we remove the fat from the stock, then add some leftover vegetables, rice and/or beans, and a dash of salt. When we come home at night, we are met by the wonderful aroma of homemade soup ready to be served.

As you can see, homemade soups don't have to take up much of your time, and the taste surpasses that of canned soup.

⊷⑤⑤⊷ PEA SOUP*

> 2 cups fresh peas (or 1 10-ounce package frozen)
> ¼ cup finely diced onion
> ⅛ teaspoon dried sweet basil
> 1 cup chicken stock

Cook the fresh peas until tender or prepare frozen peas according to the package directions. Puree the peas in a blender with the water in which they were cooked. Add the onion and basil and blend well. Combine the chicken stock with the puree and reheat to the boiling point.

Makes 4 servings.

* **Suitable for the Elimination Diet**

RECIPES

⌘ BEEF STOCK*

> 6 pounds beef soup bones
> 2½ quarts water
> 1 cup sliced onions
> ½ cup chopped celery with leaves
> 1 large bay leaf
> 4 sprigs parsley
> 8 black peppercorns
> 2 teaspoons salt

Remove the meat from the bones and cut up. Put the meat, bones, and water in a kettle. Simmer, uncovered, for 3 hours, taking care not to boil. Add the remaining ingredients. Cook, uncovered, for 2 more hours. Strain. Skim off excess fat or chill the stock and lift off the fat layer.

Makes 6 cups.

* Suitable for the Elimination Diet

⌘ CHICKEN STOCK*

> 4 pounds chicken bones or whole carcass, broken up
> 4 quarts cold water
> 1 medium onion, diced
> 1 carrot, diced
> Several stalks celery, diced
> Salt and pepper to taste

Cover the chicken bones or carcass with cold water in a heavy-bottomed saucepan. Add the onion, carrot, and celery and bring slowly to a boil. Simmer for 2 to 3 hours. Strain, season, and cool. Refrigerate. Skim off the layer of fat on top when ready to use the stock.

Makes 2 quarts.

* Suitable for the Elimination Diet

✥ CHICKEN SOUP*

1 3-pound chicken, cut up
6 cups water
2 teaspoons salt
Pepper to taste
1 bay leaf
6 carrots, cut up
1 large onion, minced
2 stalks celery, cut up
1 cup uncooked rice or barley

Place the chicken in a large stock pot. Cover with water and add the salt, pepper, and bay leaf. Cover, bring to a boil, and simmer for 1 hour, or until the chicken is tender. When the chicken is done, remove it from the stock pot. Refrigerate overnight and skim the fat from the top of the broth. Reheat the broth, add the vegetables, and cook for 35 minutes, or until the vegetables are almost tender. Skin and bone the chicken and cut the meat into small pieces. Add the chicken and rice or barley to the broth and cook for an additional 15 minutes.

Makes 8 servings.

* Suitable for the Elimination Diet

❧❦❧ CHICKEN AND POTATO SOUP*

> 2 cups chicken stock (recipe, p. 100)
> 1 cup finely diced cooked chicken
> 1 cup diced cooked potatoes, salted
> Salt to taste
> 1/4 cup minced onion
> Dried parsley flakes (optional)
> Paprika (optional)

In a heavy saucepan, combine the stock, chicken, potatoes, salt, and onion. Bring to a boil, stirring constantly. Remove from the stove and puree in a blender. Refrigerate overnight. Reheat, adding water for the desired consistency. Add salt if needed and serve with paprika or parsley sprinkled on top.

Makes 6 servings.

* **Suitable for the Elimination Diet**

❧❦❧ BEAN SOUP*

> 2 cups chicken stock (recipe, p. 100)
> 2 cups water
> 1/2 cup dried navy beans
> 1 bay leaf
> 1 cup diced carrots
> 1 cup diced celery
> 1 small onion, sliced

In a large stock pot, combine the stock and water. Bring to a boil and add the beans and bay leaf. Lower the heat and simmer the ingredients for approximately 2 hours. Remove the bay leaf and add the carrots, celery, and onion. Simmer for another 30 minutes. Force the mixture through a sieve or put it in a blender to puree. Return the soup to the pot and add enough water to thin it to the desired consistency. Reheat to boiling and serve.

Makes 6 to 8 servings.

* **Suitable for the Elimination Diet**

❧ MINESTRONE*

2 cups chopped onions
2 tablespoons oil
2 cups sliced celery
2 cups sliced carrots
4 to 6 garlic cloves, minced
2 teaspoons dried oregano
2 teaspoons dried basil
⅛ teaspoon cayenne
6 cups stock or water
3 cups cooked beans, such as pintos, kidney beans,
    limas, or soybeans (one kind or mixed together)
2 cups homemade tomato sauce (recipe, page 175) OR
    4 cups canned tomatoes
⅔ cup chopped green peppers
½ cup chopped fresh parsley
2 tablespoons wheat-free tamari
1 tablespoon apple cider vinegar
1 teaspoon honey (optional)
2 cups cooked rice

In a large 6-quart pan, sauté the onions in the oil over medium heat
for 5 minutes. Add the celery and carrots. Cook, stirring occasionally,
for 10 minutes. Add the garlic, oregano, basil, and cayenne. Cook
for another 5 minutes. Add the stock or water, beans, and tomato
sauce or tomatoes. Simmer gently for 30 minutes. Add the peppers,
parsley, tamari, vinegar, and honey. Simmer for 5 minutes. Add the
cooked rice and serve.

Makes 12 servings.

* **Suitable for the Elimination Diet**

❧ TOMATO SOUP*

> 1 6-ounce can tomato paste
> ¼ teaspoon minced onion
> 2 cups chicken stock
> ½ teaspoon salt
> ¼ cup finely chopped celery
> 1 tablespoon honey

In a large saucepan, mix all the ingredients. Bring to a boil and simmer for 5 minutes.

Makes 4 servings.

Variations, if Tolerated:
— Substitute an equal amount of sugar for the honey.
— Substitute an equal amount of milk for the chicken stock.

* **Suitable for the Elimination Diet**

❧ IRISH LAMB STEW*

> 5 pounds lamb neck chops
> Salt and pepper to taste
> 6 onions, sliced ¼ inch thick
> 6 potatoes, sliced ¼ inch thick

Preheat the oven to 300°F.

In a 3-quart casserole, put a layer of neck chops, seasoning them lightly, then a layer of onions and a layer of potatoes, seasoning again. Add enough water to almost cover the potatoes. Cover the casserole with a tight-fitting lid and bake for 3 to 4 hours, or until the lamb is tender.

Makes 4 servings.

* **Suitable for the Elimination Diet**

❧❧❧ BEEF AND VEGETABLE STEW*

2 medium potatoes, diced
2 medium carrots, sliced
⅓ cup uncooked rice
2 small onions, sliced
1 pound ground beef
1 29-ounce can whole tomatoes, drained and broken up
  (reserve liquid)
1 tablespoon maple sugar (optional)

Preheat the oven to 300°F.

Layer the vegetables and beef in the order given in a greased 2-quart casserole. Season each layer with salt and pepper. Sprinkle the reserved tomato liquid over the finished layers. Bake, covered, for 2 to 3 hours.

Makes 4 servings.

Variations:
– Just before adding the ground beef, add 1 cup cooked kidney beans (drained). Or substitute browned pure pork sausage for the ground beef.

* Suitable for the Elimination Diet

☙ VEGETABLE BEEF SOUP*

1 beef soup bone
8 cups water
1 bay leaf
1 teaspoon salt
½ teaspoon chili powder
1 cup diced potatoes
1 cup diced carrots
1 cup diced cabbage or chopped tomatoes
⅓ cup chopped onion
1 cup diced celery
2 cups cooked rice, barley, or wheat-free, corn-free noodles

Cook the bone in the water with the bay leaf, salt, and chili powder for approximately 3 hours. Add the vegetables, cover, and simmer for 1 hour more. Remove the bone and bay leaf. Remove any meat from the bone and add to the soup. Refrigerate overnight, skim off the fat, reheat, and add the rice, barley, or noodles. Cook until heated thoroughly.

Makes 12 servings.

* Suitable for the Elimination Diet

❧ CREAM OF VEGETABLE SOUP†

1/4 cup vegetable oil
3 tablespoons flour or rice flour
2 cups milk
2 cups chicken stock (recipe, p. 100)
Dash of salt and paprika
2 cups cooked vegetables and/or meat chunks

In a heavy saucepan, stir the oil and flour together over low heat. Gradually add the milk, stirring constantly. When the mixture begins to boil, add the chicken stock and continue to stir until well mixed and hot. Add the seasonings and the meat chunks, if using. Puree the vegetables in a blender, add to the soup, and cook until hot.

Makes 6 to 8 servings.

† **Free of egg, sugar, corn, citrus**

❧ CORN CHOWDER†

1 onion, diced
1 to 2 tablespoons oil
2 cups boiling water
2 cups canned corn
2 cups diced potatoes
1 teaspoon salt
Pepper to taste
2 cups milk

Cook the onion in the oil for about 5 minutes, but do not brown. Add the water, vegetables, and seasonings and cook until the potatoes are tender. Remove from the heat and slowly stir in the milk. Reheat and serve at once.

Makes 4 to 6 servings.

† **Free of egg, wheat, sugar, citrus**

ᴥᴥᴥ GREEK LEMON SOUP†

6 cups chicken stock (recipe, p. 100)
½ cup uncooked rice
Salt to taste
3 egg yolks
¼ cup lemon juice
2 tablespoons chopped fresh parsley
⅛ teaspoon cayenne

In a large pan, bring the chicken broth to a boil. Add the rice, season with salt, and cook until the rice is tender, 15 to 20 minutes. In a medium-size bowl, beat the egg yolks until light and frothy. Slowly add the lemon juice, beating well. Just before serving, dilute the egg-lemon mixture with 1 cup hot broth, beating constantly with a whisk until well blended. Gradually add the diluted mixture to the remaining hot soup, stirring constantly. Bring almost to the boiling point; do not boil or the soup will curdle. Stir in the parsley and cayenne and season to taste.

Makes 6 servings.

† **Free of milk, wheat, sugar, corn**

13 · VEGETABLES AND SIDE DISHES

Even for the person with food allergies, there is still a large selection of vegetable dishes available. Try Baked Sweet Potato Casserole, Confetti Rice, Oriental Tomato Skillet, Braised Celery, or Dilled Carrots. Besides adding valuable nutrients to your diet, they add color and variety.

✤ GREEN BEANS WITH ALMONDS*

    2 pounds green beans
    ½ teaspoon salt
    2 teaspoons finely chopped onion
    ½ cup boiling water
    ¼ cup blanched and slivered almonds
    2 tablespoons allowed oil
    ¼ cup chopped fresh parsley

Wash and dry the beans and cut into 1-inch pieces. Add the salt, onion, and beans to the boiling water. Quickly return to a boil. Reduce the heat to low and steam until tender (7 to 10 minutes). Drain the vegetables. Stir in the almonds, oil, and parsley.

Makes 6 servings.

* **Suitable for the Elimination Diet**

RECIPES

✌§§➤ DILLED CARROTS*

¾ pound carrots, sliced thin
½ cup apple juice
1½ teaspoons oil or milk-free, corn-free margarine
1 teaspoon maple syrup
2 teaspoons arrowroot
¼ cup apple juice
1 teaspoon dried dill weed

In a heavy saucepan with lid, simmer the carrots in the apple juice until tender, about 12 to 15 minutes. If the juice boils away, add a little water to prevent sticking. Add the oil (or margarine) and maple syrup. In a small bowl, mix the arrowroot and ¼ cup apple juice. Stir into the pan and cook, stirring, for 2 minutes, until the sauce is thick and clear. Stir in the dill weed.

Makes 4 to 6 servings.

Variations, if Tolerated:
– Substitute an equal amount of cornstarch for the arrowroot.

* **Suitable for the Elimination Diet**

✌§§➤ MAPLE CARROTS*

3 cups peeled and diagonally sliced carrots
¼ cup maple syrup
1 tablespoon safflower oil (optional)

Cook the carrots gently in a small amount of water. When tender crisp, add the maple syrup and, if desired, safflower oil. Simmer briefly and serve piping hot.

Makes 6 servings.

* **Suitable for the Elimination Diet**

✢ BRAISED CELERY*

1 bunch celery
4 tablespoons allowed oil
1 cup homemade chicken or beef stock (recipes, p. 100)
Salt to taste
Chopped parsley for garnish

Wash and separate the stalks of celery, removing the leaves. Cut them crosswise, on a slant, into 2-inch lengths. In a large skillet, heat the oil and sauté the celery over high heat for about 2 minutes, stirring constantly. Turn the heat down, add the stock, cover tightly, and steam for 10 minutes, or until the celery is tender but still firm. Salt to taste. Garnish with chopped parsley.

Makes 4 to 6 servings.

* Suitable for the Elimination Diet

✢ ORIENTAL TOMATO SKILLET*

2 tablespoons allowed oil
½ cup chopped onion
2 medium unpared zucchini, quartered
3 medium tomatoes, cut into wedges
1 3-ounce can sliced mushrooms, drained
Salt and pepper to taste
¼ teaspoon curry powder
¼ teaspoon ginger

Heat the oil in a wok or skillet; add the onion and zucchini. Stir-fry over medium heat for 5 minutes; stir in the remaining ingredients. Cook, covered, 5 minutes longer, or until the vegetables are tender but slightly crisp.

Makes 6 servings.

* Suitable for the Elimination Diet

RECIPES

⋙ EGGPLANT WITH TOMATO*

1½ cups cubed eggplant
2 tablespoons chopped onion
2 tablespoons chopped green pepper
2 tablespoons allowed margarine or oil
1 cup canned tomatoes
Salt and pepper to taste
¼ to ½ cup crushed puffed-rice cereal

Preheat the oven to 400°F.

Soak the eggplant in water for about 30 minutes; cook in boiling water until tender, then drain. Brown the onion and green pepper in 1 tablespoon margarine or oil; add the tomatoes and eggplant. Place in a casserole; add salt and pepper. Brown the crushed cereal in the remaining tablespoon of margarine. Sprinkle over the top of the casserole. Bake for about 15 minutes.

Makes 6 to 8 servings.

Variations, if Tolerated:
– In place of crushed puffed-rice cereal, use crushed corn flakes or cracker crumbs.

* Suitable for the Elimination Diet

⋙ CRANBERRY RELISH*

2 cups cranberries
½ cup sweet apple cider
4 tablespoons honey
½ teaspoon ground allspice
Pinch of ground cloves

Grind all ingredients together.

Makes 3 cups.

* Suitable for the Elimination Diet

❧ CONFETTI RICE*

¼ cup milk-free, corn-free margarine
1½ cups uncooked rice
3 cups hot chicken broth (recipe, p. 100)
¾ cup chopped fresh parsley
¾ cup shredded carrot
¾ cup chopped celery (1 large stalk)
¾ cup chopped green onion
¾ cup slivered toasted almonds
Sea salt and pepper to taste

Preheat the oven to 350°F.

In a heavy skillet, melt the margarine. Add the rice and toss to coat. Heat the rice in the margarine for 5 minutes, stirring occasionally. Combine the rice and chicken broth in 2-quart casserole. Cover and bake for 45 minutes. Stir in the parsley, carrot, celery, green onion, and almonds. Continue to bake for 10 minutes more.

Makes 6 to 8 servings.

* Suitable for the Elimination Diet

❧ CHINA BOWL RICE STICKS*

Rice sticks (also known as cellophane noodles) are prepared in three basic ways.

Boiled: Add 7 ounces of rice sticks to 3 quarts of rapidly boiling water. Cook for 3 minutes and drain.

Stir-fried: Soak rice sticks in hot water for 10 minutes. Drain. Cut into 2-inch lengths. Add to vegetable-meat stir-frys. Also add to soups.

Deep-fried: Drop small amounts of dry rice sticks into peanut or safflower oil heated to 375°F. The sticks will instantly puff up. Skim them off, drain, and use as a crunchy garnish. Particularly good in a chicken or tuna salad.

* Suitable for the Elimination Diet

⤙⧈⤚ RICE PILAF*

> 2 tablespoons oil
> 1 onion, chopped
> 1 ¼ cups long-grain rice
> ⅓ cup chopped dried, unsulfured apricots
> ⅓ cup seedless raisins
> ⅓ cup chopped walnuts
> 2½ cups chicken stock (recipe, p. 100)
> ½ teaspoon cinnamon (optional)
> Salt and pepper to taste

Heat the oil in a saucepan. Add the chopped onion and fry, stirring constantly, for 5 minutes, or until the onion is lightly browned. Add the rice, apricots, raisins, and walnuts. Pour the chicken stock over the rice mixture. Stir in the cinnamon and season with salt and pepper. Bring to a boil, stirring constantly. Lower the heat, cover, and simmer for 15 minutes, or until the rice is tender and the stock has been absorbed.

Makes 6 servings.

* **Suitable for the Elimination Diet**

✣ BARLEY AND MUSHROOM PILAF*

It is best to prepare this dish the day before serving so that the barley can soak overnight in the stock.

> 2 tablespoons oil
> 1 large onion, chopped
> 1 cup sliced fresh mushrooms
> ¼ cup pearl barley
> 2 cups well-seasoned chicken stock (recipe, p.100)
> Salt and pepper to taste
> 1 bay leaf

Preheat the oven to 375°F.

Heat the oil in a frying pan over medium heat. Add the chopped onion and cook, stirring frequently, for 3 minutes. Add the sliced mushrooms to the onion and fry for 1 minute, stirring constantly. Add the pearl barley and fry for 1 minute more, stirring occasionally. Transfer the barley mixture to an ovenproof dish. Pour in the stock. Season with salt and pepper. Put the bay leaf on top, cover the dish, and refrigerate for at least 2 hours, preferably overnight. Bake the casserole, covered, for 1 hour, or until the stock is absorbed and the barley is tender and slightly chewy. Serve immediately.

Makes 4 servings.

Variations, if Tolerated:
– Sprinkle with ¼ cup grated Cheddar cheese just before serving.

* **Suitable for the Elimination Diet**

⛥ HASH BROWN POTATOES*

5 to 6 medium potatoes
1 to 2 tablespoons grated onion
1 teaspoon sea salt
Dash of pepper
1/3 cup milk-free, corn-free margarine

Cook the unpeeled potatoes in water. Chill for 2 hours, then peel and shred to make 4 cups. In a large bowl, combine the potatoes, onion, salt, and pepper. Melt the margarine in a skillet. Pat the potatoes into the pan, leaving a 1/2-inch space around the edge. Cover and brown for 10 to 12 minutes. Check the potatoes, reduce the heat if necessary, and cook 8 to 10 minutes longer, until golden. Place a platter over the pan and invert to place the potatoes on it.

Makes 8 servings.

* **Suitable for the Elimination Diet**

⊰§⊱ STUFFED MUSHROOMS*

32 large fresh mushrooms
½ cup milk-free, corn-free margarine
2 tablespoons chopped walnuts
4 green onions, finely chopped
2½ tablespoons chopped fresh parsley
Salt and pepper to taste

Wash and dry the mushrooms. Remove and chop the stems. Lay the caps upside down in a well-greased 8-inch-square baking dish. In a small skillet, melt 2 tablespoons margarine. Add the mushroom stems and sauté lightly. In a small bowl, combine the stems, the remaining margarine, the onions, parsley, and salt and pepper. Mix thoroughly. Fill each cap with a rounded teaspoon of the mixture. Heat under a broiler for 3 to 5 minutes, until bubbly. Serve immediately.

Makes 6 to 8 servings.

* **Suitable for the Elimination Diet**

⊰§⊱ BAKED SWEET POTATO CASSEROLE*

½ cup maple syrup
½ cup well-drained unsweetened crushed pineapple
½ cup raisins
¼ teaspoon salt
2 cups cubed cooked sweet potatoes
2 tablespoons milk-free, corn-free margarine
¼ to ½ cup slivered almonds

Preheat the oven to 350°F.

Combine the syrup, pineapple, raisins, and salt. Arrange the potatoes in a 1-quart dish. Spread the fruit mixture on top. Dot with margarine and sprinkle with almonds. Bake for 40 to 45 minutes.

Makes 6 to 8 servings.

* **Suitable for the Elimination Diet**

✥❧ OATMEAL STUFFING†

> 1 lemon
> 1¼ cups rolled oats
> 1 tablespoon grated onion
> 1 tablespoon chopped fresh thyme
> 2 tablespoons chopped fresh parsley
> Salt and pepper to taste
> 1 egg
> 2 tablespoons milk or other liquid

Preheat the oven to 325°F.

Grate the rind of the lemon and squeeze out 1 teaspoon of lemon juice. Set aside. Combine the oats with the onion, thyme, parsley, lemon rind, and salt and pepper. Beat the egg with the milk and 1 teaspoon of lemon juice. Mix into the oat mixture, combining well. Stuff into fish, meat, or poultry or place in an ovenproof glass dish and bake for 30 minutes, until moist and tender.

Makes approximately 1¾ cups.

† **Free of wheat, sugar, corn**

14 · MAIN COURSES

One of the biggest difficulties the family cook has is to create new, interesting, and appetizing meals every day. Food allergies make the challenge even greater but not impossible.

We took our favorite recipes, made a few substitutions, and created meals that most people don't even realize are allergy-free. Try them yourself.

❧§§❧ HONEY BAKED CHICKEN*

> 2 tablespoons safflower oil
> 1 3-pound chicken, cut into serving-size pieces
> 1 teaspoon salt
> Pepper to taste
> 2 large apples, sliced
> 2 teaspoons honey
> ¼ cup apple juice

Preheat the oven to 350°F.

Heat the oil in a large skillet. Sprinkle the chicken with seasonings and brown in hot oil on all sides. Transfer to an 11-by-7-inch baking dish. Place apple slices between the chicken pieces, drizzle with honey, and pour juice over all. Cover and bake for about 50 minutes, or until the chicken is tender. Serve hot.

Makes 6 servings.

* Suitable for the Elimination Diet

❦ BAKED CHICKEN WITH TOMATO RICE STUFFING*

        2 pounds chicken, cut up
        2 tablespoons oil
        1/3 cup chopped celery
        1/4 cup chopped green pepper
        1/3 cup chopped onion
        2/3 cup uncooked rice
        1 cup chopped tomatoes
        1/2 cup water
        3/4 teaspoon salt
        Dash of pepper
        1/4 teaspoon sage

Preheat the oven to 350°F.

Brown the chicken in oil in a heavy skillet. While the chicken browns, combine the celery, green pepper, onion, rice, and tomatoes in a mixing bowl. Turn the mixture into an 11-by-7-inch baking dish. Arrange the chicken on the rice. Sprinkle with additional salt, pepper, and sage. Cover and bake for 1 hour, or until the chicken is tender.

Makes 6 servings.

* Suitable for the Elimination Diet

✎↫ CHICKEN SUPREME*

> 3 medium-size chicken breasts, halved, OR 6 chicken
>   thighs
> ½ teaspoon salt
> Dash of paprika
> ½ teaspoon curry powder
> Dash of pepper
> 1¼ cups chicken stock (recipe, p. 100)

Preheat the oven to 350°F.

Sprinkle the chicken with salt and paprika. Place in an 11-by-7-inch baking dish. Add the curry powder and pepper to the chicken stock and stir. Pour over the chicken. Cover with foil and bake for 30 minutes. Remove the foil and bake 45 minutes longer. Remove the chicken to a warm platter. Strain the pan juices and reserve for the mushroom sauce.

Mushroom Sauce

> 3 tablespoons oat flour
> ¼ cup cold water
> Reserved pan juices
> 1 3-ounce can sliced mushrooms, drained

Blend the flour with cold water in a saucepan. Slowly stir in the reserved pan juices. Cook and stir over low heat until the sauce thickens and bubbles. Boil for 3 to 4 minutes longer, then add the mushrooms. Heat thoroughly. Spoon the sauce over the chicken.

Makes 6 servings.

Variations, if Tolerated:
– Substitute 2½ tablespoons cornstarch or wheat flour for the oat flour.

* Suitable for the Elimination Diet

◆⅀ℰ◆ CHICKEN OR TURKEY LOAF*

> 1 cup chicken stock (recipe, p. 100)
> 1 cup crushed rice crackers
> 2 tablespoons milk-free, egg-free margarine
> 3 cups finely chopped or ground cooked chicken or
>   turkey
> ½ cup chopped celery
> 3 tablespoons finely chopped onion
> 2 teaspoons sage
> 1 teaspoon salt
> ¼ teaspoon pepper

Preheat the oven to 325°F.

In a large bowl, mix all the ingredients together thoroughly and pat into a greased loaf pan. Bake for 1 hour, or until done.

Makes 6 servings.

Variations, if Tolerated:
– Mix 2 eggs with the rest of the ingredients.
– Substitute wheat crackers for the rice crackers.

* **Suitable for the Elimination Diet**

⋖⋟⋗ SLOPPY JOES*

> 1½ pounds ground beef
> 3 tablespoons apple cider vinegar
> 4 tablespoons unsweetened pineapple juice
> 3 tablespoons maple sugar
> 1 cup corn-free, sugar-free tomato sauce (recipe, p. 175)
> ½ cup water
> ¼ cup chopped green pepper (optional)
> ¼ cup chopped onion (optional)
> Salt and pepper to taste

Brown the ground beef in a skillet. Drain off excess fat. Add the remaining ingredients. Cover and simmer for 20 minutes. Serve on an allowed bread or buns.

Makes 6 sandwiches.

Variations, if Tolerated:
– Substitute an equal amount of sugar for the maple sugar.
– Substitute 1 tablespoon lemon juice for the pineapple juice.

* Suitable for the Elimination Diet

☙§❧ QUICK SAVORY MEAT LOAF*

2 pounds ground beef
⅓ cup Minute Tapioca
⅓ cup finely chopped onion
1½ teaspoons salt
¼ teaspoon pepper
¼ teaspoon savory (optional)
1 12-ounce can tomatoes, broken up

Preheat the oven to 350°F.

In a large bowl, combine all the ingredients. Mix well. Spoon into a 9-by-5-inch loaf pan. Press in lightly. Bake for 1 to 1¼ hours. *Makes 8 servings.*

* **Suitable for the Elimination Diet**

❦ BROILED BURGERS*

I pound ground beef
½ teaspoon salt
Dash of pepper
¼ cup corn-free, sugar-free tomato sauce (recipe,
    p. 175)
¼ cup chopped green pepper
¼ cup chopped onion
¼ cup chopped sunflower seeds
4 thick slices tomato

Combine the ground beef, salt, pepper, tomato sauce, onion, and sunflower seeds. Shape into four patties. Broil to the desired doneness. Top each burger with a tomato slice before serving.

Makes 4 servings.

* **Suitable for the Elimination Diet**

❦ PORK CHOP SPANISH RICE*

6 pork chops, ½ inch thick
1½ teaspoons salt
½ to 1 teaspoon chili powder
Dash of pepper
¾ cup long-grain rice
½ cup chopped onion
3½ cups canned whole tomatoes with juice

Brown the pork chops. Drain off excess fat. Combine the seasonings and sprinkle over the meat. Add the rice, onion, and tomatoes. Cover and cook over low heat for 45 minutes to 1 hour, spooning the liquid over the rice occasionally.

Makes 6 servings.

* **Suitable for the Elimination Diet**

❧❦❧ PINEAPPLE PORK CHOPS WITH RICE*

> 4 pork chops, ½ inch to ¾ inch thick
> Salt and pepper
> 1 8-ounce can unsweetened crushed pineapple
> 1 cup water
> ¾ teaspoon salt
> 1½ cups cooked rice

Sprinkle the pork chops with salt and pepper. In a large skillet, brown the pork chops on both sides. Add the pineapple and reduce the heat. Cover and simmer until tender, about 30 minutes. Move the chops to the side of the pan. Add the water and salt. Bring to a full boil and stir in the rice. Remove from the heat. Cover and let stand for 5 minutes.

Makes 4 servings.

* Suitable for the Elimination Diet

❧§❧ LAMB PILAF*

3 pounds lamb stew meat
6 cups lamb stock or water
2 garlic cloves, minced
1 teaspoon basil
1 teaspoon oregano
1 teaspoon rosemary
Salt and pepper to taste
¼ cup minced onion
2½ tablespoons oil
1½ cups uncooked brown rice
½ cup slivered blanched almonds
3 tablespoons oil
⅔ cup raisins
1 green pepper, sliced into rings

Cut the lamb into 1½-inch cubes, trimming away fat. Simmer lamb bones, if desired, for 1 to 2 hours to make stock. Put the lamb, stock or water, garlic, and seasonings into a pot and simmer for 1 hour, or until the lamb is tender. Lift out the lamb and set aside. Strain the stock. Sauté the minced onions in oil until tender. Add the brown rice and stir. Add 4 cups strained stock, stir, and cover tightly. Simmer over medium heat until the stock is absorbed and the rice is tender, about 35 to 40 minutes. Toss the lamb and rice together gently and serve.

Prepare a garnish by sautéing the almonds lightly in oil until golden and remove with a slotted spoon. Then sauté the raisins in the same pan with more oil, if necessary, until they are puffy. Scatter the almonds and raisins over the lamb and rice. Top with thin slices of raw green pepper.

Makes 6 to 8 servings.

* Suitable for the Elimination Diet

🍃 CHICKEN CHOP SUEY*

1 cup chopped celery
½ cup chopped onions
½ cup chopped green peppers
1 cup sliced mushrooms
2½ tablespoons oil
2 cups 1-inch strips cooked chicken or pork
2 cups chicken stock (recipe, p. 100)
2 tablespoons wheat-free tamari
2 tablespoons arrowroot
¼ cup cold water
1 cup fresh sprouts (try mung beans or soybeans)

In a wok or heavy-bottomed skillet, sauté the celery, onions, green peppers, and mushrooms in oil until just tender. Add the chicken or pork, chicken stock, and tamari and simmer while stirring constantly. Dissolve the arrowroot in cold water and add gradually, stirring until it is cooked and the chop suey is thickened. Add raw bean sprouts just before serving.

Makes 6 servings.

Variations, if Tolerated:
– In place of arrowroot, use 2 tablespoons cornstarch.

* **Suitable for the Elimination Diet**

❧ CHERRY AND ORANGE DUCK†

This quick and easy recipe is a nice alternative to chicken or turkey.

> 1 onion
> 1 4-pound duck
> Salt and pepper
> 1 pound cherries
> Grated rind of 1 orange
> Juice of 2 oranges
> ¾ cup chicken stock

Preheat the oven to 400°F.

Cut the onion in half and place in the cavity of the duck. Put the duck on a rack in a roasting pan. Prick the skin all over with a fork to allow the fat to run out. Rub the skin with salt. Roast the duck for about 1 hour. Pit the cherries and put them in a bowl. Add the grated orange rind plus the orange juice. When the duck has cooked for an hour, drain off the fat that has collected in the roasting pan. Remove the rack and put the duck back in the pan. Pour the cherries and orange juice around the duck with the chicken stock. Cover the pan with foil and roast for 30 minutes more. Remove the duck to a warmed serving platter. Drain half of the cherries in the pan and put them around the duck and keep it warm.

For the sauce, put the remaining cherries into a blender or food processor with the cooking liquid and blend until smooth. Reheat the sauce, season to taste with salt and pepper, and serve with the duck.

Makes 8 servings.

† **Free of milk, egg, wheat, sugar, corn**

RECIPES

❧❧❧ FISH AMANDINE†

1½ teaspoons oil, such as almond oil
½ cup slivered or chopped almonds
1½ pounds fish fillets
2 tablespoons lemon juice (optional)

In a small saucepan, heat the oil and sauté the nuts until lightly browned. Set the saucepan aside. Cook the fish in a nonstick frying pan until it is opaque and flakes easily with a fork. Return the almonds to the heat. Add the lemon juice and warm thoroughly. Pour over the fish.

Makes 4 servings.

† **Free of milk, egg, wheat, sugar, corn**

❧❧❧ FLOUNDER FLORENTINE†

¼ cup chopped onion
⅛ teaspoon crushed dill
2 tablespoons oil
1½ pounds fresh spinach, chopped
½ cup cooked brown rice
⅓ cup chopped toasted almonds
1 tablespoon lemon juice
6 flounder fillets (about 1½ pounds)

Preheat the oven to 350°F. Oil a shallow 10-by-6-inch baking dish.

In a saucepan, sauté the onion and dill in oil until tender. Add the spinach and sauté just enough to wilt it. Add the rice, almonds, and lemon juice. Heat, stirring occasionally. Place ¼ cup of the mixture on each fish fillet. Roll up and press the ends securely. Arrange on a baking dish and bake for 20 minutes. If desired, serve with Mushroom Sauce (recipe, p. 121).

Makes 6 servings.

† **Free of milk, egg, wheat, sugar, corn**

15 · COOKIES, BARS, FRUIT TREATS, AND SNACKS

When my children were younger, I would try to have a nutritious snack ready for them when they came home from school. Let your children look forward to some of these special goodies.

COOKIES AND BARS

❧ BANANA OATMEAL COOKIES*

½ cup maple sugar
¾ cup milk-free, corn-free margarine
1⅓ cups mashed ripe bananas
4 cups rolled oats
1 cup raisins OR ½ cup raisins and ½ cup chopped nuts

Preheat the oven to 325°F. Grease a cookie sheet.

In a large bowl, cream together the sugar and margarine. Stir in the bananas. Add the rolled oats and raisins and mix well. Drop by the teaspoonful 2 inches apart onto a greased cookie sheet. Bake for 20 minutes.

Makes 72 cookies.

Variations, if Tolerated:
— Substitute an equal amount of sugar for the maple sugar.
— Substitute 1 cup wheat flour for 1 cup of the rolled oats.
— Add 1 egg to the creamed sugar and margarine.

* Suitable for the Elimination Diet

❧❀❧ ALMOND CRESCENTS*

> 1⅓ cups potato starch
> ⅓ cup maple sugar
> ¼ teaspoon sea salt
> 2 teaspoons baking powder
> ¼ cup milk-free, corn-free margarine
> ⅓ cup nut milk
> ½ teaspoon vanilla
> ½ cup shredded coconut or crushed almonds

Preheat the oven to 350°F. Grease a cookie sheet.

Place the dry ingredients in a bowl and cut in the margarine. Add the nut milk and vanilla, working the dough into a soft, smooth consistency that holds together without being sticky. Add coconut or almonds. Form into small crescents and place 2 inches apart on the cookie sheet. Bake for 12 to 15 minutes.

Makes 24 cookies.

Variations, if Tolerated:
— Substitute an equal amount of sugar for the maple sugar.
— Substitute 2 cups wheat flour for the potato starch.
— Substitute an equal amount of milk for the nut milk.

* Suitable for the Elimination Diet

❧❀❧ ALMOND COOKIES*

> 2 cups finely ground almonds
> ½ cup honey
> ½ teaspoon sea salt
> ¼ cup water
> 3 tablespoons carob powder (optional)

Preheat the oven to 350°F. Grease a cookie sheet.

Grind the nuts in a blender, being careful not to overgrind. Mix with the remaining ingredients. Drop by the teaspoonful 2 inches apart onto a greased cookie sheet. Bake for 10 to 12 minutes. Place whole almonds on top of each cookie for decoration.

Makes 24 cookies.

* Suitable for the Elimination Diet

⋐§℥⋑ RAISIN NUT COOKIES*

⅓ cup milk-free, corn-free margarine
½ cup honey or maple syrup OR ⅔ cup maple sugar
1 teaspoon vanilla
¼ cup soy flour
½ cup rice flour
½ cup potato starch flour
¼ teaspoon sea salt
½ teaspoon baking soda
¼ to ½ cup raisins
¼ to ½ cup chopped nuts

Preheat the oven to 375°F.

In a large bowl, cream the margarine, honey, and vanilla. Sift the dry ingredients together and add to the honey mixture. Mix well. Stir in the nuts and raisins. Drop by the teaspoonful 2 inches apart onto an ungreased cookie sheet. Bake for 10 to 12 minutes.

Makes 48 cookies.

Variations, if Tolerated:
— Substitute an equal amount of sugar for the honey.
— Use 1 cup wheat flour in place of the other flours.

* Suitable for the Elimination Diet

❧❦❧ BLUEBERRY DELIGHT COOKIES*

⅓ cup milk-free, corn-free margarine
⅔ cup maple sugar
1 tablespoon coconut milk
1 teaspoon vanilla
¼ teaspoon sea salt
½ teaspoon baking powder
1 cup rice flour
¼ cup unsweetened applesauce
¼ cup fresh blueberries

Preheat the oven to 350°F. Grease a cookie sheet.

In a large bowl, cream the margarine and sugar until fluffy. Add the coconut milk and vanilla and beat until smooth. Beat in all the other ingredients except the blueberries. Gently fold in the berries by hand. Drop by the teaspoonful 2 inches apart onto a greased cookie sheet. Bake 10 to 14 minutes.

Makes 48 cookies.

Variations, if Tolerated:

— Substitute an equal amount of sugar for the maple sugar.
— Substitute 1¼ cups wheat flour for the rice flour.
— Add 1 egg to the creamed sugar and margarine and omit the applesauce.
— Substitute an equal amount of milk for the coconut milk.

* Suitable for the Elimination Diet

❧❦❧ PECAN BALLS*

⅓ cup milk-free, corn-free margarine
⅓ cup maple sugar
1 tablespoon water or nut milk
1 teaspoon vanilla
¼ teaspoon sea salt
½ teaspoon baking powder
1 cup rice flour
¼ cup finely chopped pecans or coconut

Preheat the oven to 350°F.

Mix together all the ingredients except the pecans and form by hand into balls. Dip the balls in water or nut milk and roll in the pecans or coconut. Place on ungreased cookie sheets 1 inch apart. Bake for 8 to 10 minutes.

Makes 36 cookies.

Variations, if Tolerated:

— Substitute an equal amount of sugar for the maple sugar.
— Roll the pecan balls in well-beaten egg instead of water.
— Substitute 1 tablespoon milk for the water.

* Suitable for the Elimination Diet

⋙ APPLESAUCE COOKIES*

> ¼ cup milk-free, corn-free margarine
> ½ cup maple sugar or maple syrup
> ⅓ cup unsweetened thick applesauce
> ¼ teaspoon vanilla
> 1 cup potato starch
> ¼ teaspoon sea salt
> 2 teaspoons baking powder
> ¼ cup chopped nuts

Preheat the oven to 350°F. Grease a cookie sheet.

In a large bowl, cream the margarine and sugar or syrup together. Add the applesauce and vanilla. Sift together the dry ingredients and stir into the maple mixture. Add the nuts. Drop by the teaspoonful 2 inches apart onto a greased cookie sheet. Bake for about 12 minutes.

Makes 24 cookies.

Variations, if Tolerated:
— Substitute an equal amount of sugar for the maple sugar.
— Substitute 1½ cups wheat flour for the potato starch.

* Suitable for the Elimination Diet

⋙ BUTTERSCOTCH COOKIES*

> ⅓ cup milk-free, corn-free margarine
> ⅓ cup honey
> 1 teaspoon vanilla
> ¼ teaspoon sea salt
> ½ teaspoon baking powder
> 1 cup rolled oats
> ¼ cup oat flour
> ½ cup finely chopped almonds

Preheat the oven to 350°F. Grease a cookie sheet.

In a large bowl, cream the margarine and honey until fluffy. Add the vanilla and beat until smooth. Beat in all the other ingredients.

Drop by the teaspoonful 3 inches apart onto a well-greased cookie sheet. Bake for 8 to 10 minutes or until light brown. Let cool completely before removing from the sheet.

Makes 36 cookies.

Variations, if Tolerated:
– Substitute an equal amount of sugar for the honey.
– Use ½ cup wheat flour and ¾ cup rolled oats in place of the 1 cup rolled oats and ¼ cup oat flour.
– Add 1 egg to the creamed margarine and honey.

* Suitable for the Elimination Diet

❦ MAPLE OATMEAL COOKIES*

> 1 cup oat flour
> ¼ teaspoon sea salt
> 1 teaspoon baking powder
> 1 cup rolled oats
> ½ cup chopped walnuts
> ½ cup milk-free, corn-free margarine
> Egg replacer equivalent to 1 egg
> ¾ cup maple sugar
> 1½ teaspoons vanilla

Preheat the oven to 400°F. Grease a cookie sheet.

Sift together the oat flour, salt, and baking powder. Add the oats and chopped walnuts. Mix well and set aside. Cream the margarine with the egg replacer. Add the maple sugar and vanilla and mix well. Combine all the ingredients. Drop by the teaspoonful 2 inches apart onto a greased cookie sheet. Bake for 8 to 12 minutes.

Makes 72 cookies.

Variations, if Tolerated:
– Substitute 1 egg for the egg replacer.
– Substitute an equal amount of sugar for the maple sugar
– Substitute 1 cup wheat flour for the oat flour.

* Suitable for the Elimination Diet

❧❧❧ PEANUT BUTTER GRANOLA BARS*

2 tablespoons safflower oil
1 cup rolled oats
1 cup mixed nuts
⅓ cup unsweetened grated coconut
¼ teaspoon sea salt
1 cup chunky or plain peanut butter or other nut butter
¾ cup honey
¾ cup fruit juice, water, nut milk, or goat's milk
1 teaspoon pure vanilla
1 teaspoon xanthan gum (optional)
¼ cup banana flakes OR 1 small ripe banana

Preheat the oven to 325°F. Grease a 9-by-13-inch pan.

Heat the oil in a large saucepan. Add the oats, nuts, coconut, and salt. Toast lightly over medium heat, stirring constantly. In a small mixing bowl, combine the peanut butter, honey, juice, vanilla, xanthan gum, and banana flakes. Add to the oat and nut mixture. Cook for about 5 minutes, stirring constantly. Spread the mixture in the greased pan and bake for 25 to 30 minutes. Cool and cut into bars.

Makes 15 bars.

Variations, if Tolerated:
- Substitute an equal amount of sugar for the honey.
- Use ½ cup wheat flour and ¾ cup rolled oats in place of the 1 cup rolled oats.
- Add 1 egg to the peanut butter mixture and omit the xanthan gum.

* Suitable for the Elimination Diet

❦ BARLEY DROP COOKIES†

⅓ cup milk-free, corn-free margarine
¾ cup sugar
1½ teaspoons pure vanilla
2 cups barley flour
1 tablespoon baking powder
½ teaspoon salt
½ cup water, nut milk, or goat's milk

Preheat the oven to 350°F. Grease a cookie sheet.

Cream the margarine and sugar and stir in the vanilla. Add the dry ingredients alternately with ½ cup water. Blend well. Drop by the teaspoonful onto a greased cookie sheet and bake for 12 to 14 minutes.

Makes about 56 cookies.

† **Free of milk, egg, wheat, corn, citrus**

ໝໝ BROWNIES†

> 2 ounces (squares) unsweetened chocolate
> ⅓ cup shortening
> 2 eggs
> ½ teaspoon salt
> 1 cup sugar
> 1 cup rice flour
> ½ teaspoon vanilla
> ½ cup chopped walnuts (optional)

Preheat the oven to 350°F. Grease an 8-inch-square pan.

Melt the chocolate and shortening over hot water. Set aside to cool. Beat the eggs until foamy. Add salt and beat until thick. Add the sugar gradually and continue beating until pale yellow. Blend in the cooled chocolate and shortening mixture. Add the flour, vanilla, and nuts. Stir until smooth. Spread into the greased pan. Bake for 35 to 40 minutes. Cool slightly and cut into squares.

Makes about 9 brownies.

Variations, if Tolerated:
– Substitute 1¼ cups wheat flour for the rice flour.

† **Free of milk, wheat, corn, citrus**

FRUIT TREATS

⊸ఫ఼ APPLE CRISP*

3 cups peeled, sliced or chopped apples
1 tablespoon oat or rice flour
2 tablespoons maple syrup
1 teaspoon cinnamon (optional)
⅛ teaspoon sea salt
1 tablespoon water
½ cup rolled oats
¼ teaspoon sea salt
¼ cup milk-free, corn-free margarine
⅓ cup maple sugar

Preheat the oven to 375°F. Grease an 8-inch-square casserole dish.
   Combine the apples, flour, maple syrup, cinnamon, salt, and water.
Put into the casserole dish. Mix together the oats, salt, margarine,
and maple sugar. Sprinkle on top of the apple mixture. Bake for 35
to 45 minutes.

Makes 8 servings.

Variation:
– Add ¼ cup peanut butter to the topping and reduce the margarine
   to 2 tablespoons.

* **Suitable for the Elimination Diet**

৶৳৶ APPLESAUCE*

        4 medium apples
        ½ cup honey
        2 tablespoons pineapple, apple, or pear juice

Wash and core the apples and cut into small pieces. Place all the ingredients in a blender and process to the desired texture.

Makes 4 servings.

Variations, if Tolerated:
− Substitute an equal amount of sugar for the honey.

* Suitable for the Elimination Diet

৶৳৶ APPLE RICE BETTY*

        1 cup honey
        ¼ teaspoon cloves (optional)
        ¼ teaspoon cinnamon (optional)
        ¼ teaspoon sea salt
        1 cup cooked rice
        4 large tart apples, peeled, cored, and thinly sliced
        ½ cup chopped walnuts
        ¼ cup oil

Preheat the oven to 350°F. Grease an 11-by-7-inch baking dish.

Mix the honey with the spices and salt. Place a thin layer of rice in the baking dish. Add a layer of thinly sliced apples and sprinkle with the honey, spices, and nuts. Repeat the layers until all the ingredients are used (ending with honey and nuts on top). Pour oil over all. Bake until the apples are soft. Serve hot.

Makes 10 servings.

Variations, if Tolerated:
− Substitute an equal amount of sugar for the honey.

* Suitable for the Elimination Diet

✦✦✦ FRENCH-FRIED BANANAS*

4 medium green bananas
⅓ cup allowed oil
½ teaspoon sea salt

Peel the bananas and cut in halves crosswise. Cut each half into six strips. Heat the oil in a 10-inch skillet over medium heat. Add a single layer of banana strips and fry until the edges are golden brown. Remove with a slotted spoon and drain on paper towels. Repeat with the remaining banana strips. Sprinkle lightly with salt. Serve at once.

Makes 4 servings.

* **Suitable for the Elimination Diet**

✦✦✦ PINEAPPLE PORCUPINES*

1 whole fresh pineapple
1 cup honey
1 cup sunflower or sesame seeds

Pare and core the pineapple. Cut it into pieces about 2 inches square. Insert a toothpick into each square. In a saucepan, warm the honey but do not boil. Dip the pineapple squares into the honey and roll them in seeds. If desired, put them in the freezer to harden. The ingredients may be served separately as a "do-it-yourself" snack.

Makes 8 to 9 servings.

* **Suitable for the Elimination Diet**

❧❧❧ JAMAICAN BAKED BANANAS*

4 to 6 bananas (sliced if desired)
2 tablespoons allowed margarine
2 tablespoons maple sugar
⅞ cup pineapple or apple juice
2 tablespoons tapioca flour
2 tablespoons pineapple or apple juice
¼ to ½ cup raisins (optional)
Grated coconut

Preheat the oven to 350°F.

Peel the bananas and arrange in an 8-inch-square casserole dish. Combine the margarine, sugar, and juice in a saucepan, bring to a boil, and cook about 1 minute, stirring constantly. Combine the tapioca flour with 2 tablespoons juice and add to the hot mixture. Cook until clear and thick. Add raisins. Pour over the bananas. Top with grated coconut. Bake for 25 to 30 minutes.

Makes 4 to 5 servings.

Variations, if Tolerated:
– Substitute an equal amount of sugar for the maple sugar.
– Substitute wheat flour for the tapioca flour.

* **Suitable for the Elimination Diet**

❧❧❧ BAKED PEARS*

4 pears
¼ to ½ cup maple syrup or honey

Preheat the oven to 350°F.

Pare, halve, and core the pears. Arrange in a greased baking dish, drizzle with maple syrup or honey, and bake 15 to 20 minutes, or until the pears are tender.

Makes 4 servings.

* **Suitable for the Elimination Diet**

⊰⧂⧁⊱ FROSTY FREEZER TREATS*

2 peeled medium bananas
½ cup pure peanut butter
¼ cup nut milk
2 tablespoons honey
½ cup chopped toasted almonds

Cut the bananas into halves or thirds crosswise and insert popsicle sticks into the ends. Place on a cookie sheet and freeze. Blend the peanut butter with the nut milk and honey until smooth. Coat the frozen banana pieces with the peanut butter mixture and roll in almonds to cover. Return to the freezer to harden. Wrap in plastic bags before storing in freezer.

Makes 4 to 6 fruit treats.

Variations, if Tolerated:
— Substitute an equal amount of milk for the nut milk.

* Suitable for the Elimination Diet

⊰⧂⧁⊱ CANTALOUPE SHERBET*

1½ cups water
½ cup honey
3 cups fresh cantaloupe pulp and juice

Boil the water and honey together for about 5 minutes, until the honey dissolves. Put the cantaloupe pulp and juice in a blender and puree well. Add honey and water mixture and blend well. Pour into ice cube trays. Freeze until firm.

Makes 6 servings.

Variations, if Tolerated:
— Substitute an equal amount of sugar for the honey.

* Suitable for the Elimination Diet

✒️ FRUIT SHERBET*

⅔ cup tapioca flour
⅔ cup honey
3 cups water
1 quart blueberries or strawberries, sliced
1 teaspoon vanilla

Mix the tapioca flour, honey, and water in a small saucepan and bring to a boil. Cook over medium heat, stirring constantly, until thick. Remove from the heat and stir in the fruit and vanilla. Puree in a blender until smooth. Pour into freezer trays. Freeze until firm.

Makes 2 quarts.

* **Suitable for the Elimination Diet**

✒️ WATERMELON SHERBET*

2 to 4 cups cubed watermelon, seeds removed
½ to 1 tablespoon honey

Put the watermelon in a blender and puree well. Add a little honey if desired. Pour into ice cube trays or pint jars and freeze.

Makes 4 servings.

Variations, if Tolerated:
– Substitute an equal amount of sugar for the honey.

* **Suitable for the Elimination Diet**

SNACKS

✥⟨⟩✥ CAROB CANDY*

Have everything ready before you begin.

> 1 cup honey
> ⅓ cup carob powder
> Dash of sea salt
> 2 tablespoons milk-free, corn-free margarine
> 2 teaspoons vanilla
> ½ cup peanut butter or other nut butter
> 3 cups rolled oats

Boil the honey, carob powder, salt, and margarine for 1 minute. Remove from the heat and add the vanilla, peanut butter, and oats. Stir quickly and drop by the teaspoonful onto waxed paper to cool. Makes 72 pieces.

Variations, if Tolerated:
– Substitute an equal amount of sugar for the honey.

* **Suitable for the Elimination Diet**

✥⟨⟩✥ COCONUT-COVERED RAISINS*

> ½ cup honey
> 4 cups raisins
> 1 cup toasted, finely grated, unsweetened coconut

Warm the honey and stir in the raisins. Lift them out with a slotted spoon and drop into the coconut. Mix until well coated and spread on waxed paper. Separate and cool.

Makes 5 cups.

* **Suitable for the Elimination Diet**

◆◇◆ QUICK BANANA OATMEAL CRISP*

    2 to 3 cups rolled oats
    4 medium bananas
    4 tablespoons honey

Preheat the oven to 250°F.

    Cover a nonstick cookie sheet with a thin layer of oats. Blend or mash the bananas and honey thoroughly. Drizzle the mixture over the oats and bake until leathery (about 1 hour). Cool, then tear apart.

Makes 2 to 3 servings.

* **Suitable for the Elimination Diet**

◆◇◆ APPLE SNACK*

    2 pounds apples

Preheat the oven to 225°F.

    Peel, core, and halve the apples. Shred coarsely and put on a buttered cookie sheet. Bake until dry. Remove from the cookie sheet with a pancake turner. Break into pieces. Store in an airtight container.

* **Suitable for the Elimination Diet**

16 · CAKES, PIES, AND PUDDINGS

For those special occasions, we have created some unusual and delicious pies and cakes.

Try Pumpkin Pecan Pie for Thanksgiving or serve Banana Cake at a birthday party. Of course, you don't have to wait until a holiday to try these recipes.

CAKES

～§Ᏸ～ FRUITY SPICE CAKE*

    1 cup water
    2 cups raisins
    1 cup maple sugar
    ½ cup milk-free, corn-free margarine
    ½ teaspoon cinnamon
    ½ teaspoon allspice
    ⅛ teaspoon nutmeg
    ½ teaspoon sea salt
    1½ cups potato starch or rice flour
    2 teaspoons baking powder
    1 teaspoon baking soda
    1 cup chopped pecans (optional)

Preheat the oven to 375°F. Grease a 9-inch-square pan.

In a medium-size saucepan, bring the water, raisins, sugar, margarine, spices, and salt to a boil. Simmer, uncovered, for 3 minutes. Let cool. Sift together the flour, baking powder, and baking soda. Stir in the raisin mixture and nuts. Beat until smooth. Pour into the baking dish and bake for 35 to 40 minutes. Cool in pan for 15 minutes. Turn out of pan and cool completely.

Makes 9 to 10 servings.

Variations, if Tolerated:
— Substitute an equal amount of sugar for the maple sugar.
— Substitute an equal amount of milk for the water.
— Substitute 2 cups wheat flour for the rice flour.
— Add 1 egg to the cooled raisin-margarine mixture.

* Suitable for the Elimination Diet

❧ RICE SPICE CAKE*

1 cup honey
¾ cup water
⅓ cup milk-free, corn-free margarine
1 cup raisins
½ teaspoon sea salt
½ teaspoon cinnamon
½ teaspoon nutmeg
2¼ cups sifted rice flour
1½ teaspoons baking powder

Preheat the oven to 325°F. Grease an 8-by-4-inch loaf pan.

Combine the first five ingredients in a medium-size saucepan, bring to a boil, reduce the heat, and simmer for 3 minutes, stirring constantly. Remove from the heat. Sift together the spices, flour, and baking powder. Add to the raisin mixture and beat well. Pour into the loaf pan and bake for 1 hour.

Makes 8 to 9 servings.

Variations, if Tolerated:
— Substitute an equal amount of sugar for the honey.
— Substitute an equal amount of milk for the water.
— Substitute 2¾ cups wheat flour for the rice flour.
— Add 1 egg to the cooled raisin-margarine mixture.

* Suitable for the Elimination Diet

❦ OATMEAL RAISIN CARROT CAKE*

1 cup honey
1 cup water or nut milk
⅓ cup milk-free, corn-free margarine
½ cup raisins
1 cup grated carrots
½ teaspoon nutmeg (optional)
2 teaspoons cinnamon (optional)
1 teaspoon baking soda
1 teaspoon sea salt
2 teaspoons water
2½ cups oat flour OR 1¾ cups rice flour
2½ teaspoons baking powder
½ cup chopped nuts

Preheat the oven to 350°F. Grease an 8-by-4-inch loaf pan.

Mix the honey, water, margarine, raisins, carrots, and spices in a saucepan. Bring to a boil and simmer for 3 minutes. Cool to luke-warm. Mix together the baking soda, salt, and water and add to the honey mixture. Mix the flour and baking powder together and stir in. Fold in the nuts. Pour into the loaf pan and bake for 50 minutes.

Makes 6 servings.

Variations, if Tolerated:
– Substitute an equal amount of sugar for the honey.
– Substitute an equal amount of milk for the water or nut milk.
– Substitute 2 cups wheat flour for the rice flour.
– Add 1 egg to the cooled raisin-margarine mixture.

* Suitable for the Elimination Diet

✎§§✎ WACKY "CHOCOLATE" CAKE*

1½ cups rice flour
2 heaping tablespoons carob powder
¼ teaspoon sea salt
1 teaspoon baking soda
1 cup maple sugar
½ cup safflower oil
1 teaspoon vanilla
1 cup warm water, nut milk, or goat's milk

Preheat the oven to 350°F.

Sift together the flour, carob powder, salt, baking soda, and sugar. Heap the dry ingredients into an ungreased 9-inch-square pan. In a small bowl, mix together the oil, vanilla, and water. Make a well in the center of the flour mixture, gently pour in the liquid, and mix. Bake for 40 minutes.

Makes 9 to 10 servings.

Variations, if Tolerated:
— Substitute an equal amount of sugar for the maple sugar.
— Substitute an equal amount of milk for the water or nut milk.
— Substitute 2 cups wheat flour for the rice flour.
— Substitute an equal amount of cocoa for the carob.

* Suitable for the Elimination Diet

ᏋᏪᏋᏊ BANANA CAKE*

2 cups oat flour
½ teaspoon sea salt
2 teaspoons baking powder
2 teaspoons safflower oil
½ cup mashed banana
½ cup maple syrup or honey
Egg replacer equal to 2 eggs
3 tablespoons cold water

Preheat the oven to 350°F. Grease an 8-inch-square pan.

Mix together the flour, salt, and baking powder. Add the oil, banana, syrup, egg replacer, and water. Mix well. Turn into the baking dish and bake for 25 to 30 minutes.

Makes 6 servings.

Variations, if Tolerated:
– Substitute an equal amount of sugar for the honey.
– Substitute an equal amount of milk for the water.
– Substitute 1¾ cups wheat flour for the oat flour.
– Substitute 2 eggs for the egg replacer.

* Suitable for the Elimination Diet

✙✙✙ TAPIOCA PINEAPPLE CAKE*

    1¾ cups tapioca flour
    ½ teaspoon baking powder
    ¼ teaspoon salt
    ½ to 1 cup honey
    ½ cup safflower oil
    1¼ cups drained, crushed pineapple (reserve liquid)
    1 tablespoon vanilla

Preheat the oven to 350°F. Grease and flour (with tapioca flour) two 8-inch cake pans.

Mix together the dry ingredients. Combine the honey, safflower oil, drained pineapple, and vanilla and mix well. Add the liquid ingredients to the dry ingredients. Add the pineapple liquid and extra water as needed to bring to the consistency of cake batter. Pour into prepared cake pans and bake for 25 to 35 minutes. Cool. Frost with Blender Broiled Frosting (recipe, page 158), if desired.

Makes 8 to 9 servings.

Variations, if Tolerated:
— Substitute an equal amount of sugar for the honey.
— Substitute 1¾ cups wheat flour for the tapioca flour.
— Add 1 egg to the pineapple liquid.

* Suitable for the Elimination Diet

❧❧ BUTTERSCOTCH CHIFFON TUBE CAKE†

1¾ cups barley flour
½ cup tapioca flour
4 teaspoons baking powder
1 teaspoon salt
½ cup vegetable oil
5 medium egg yolks
½ cup cold water
2 teaspoons vanilla extract
¾ cup maple syrup or honey
1 cup egg whites (7 or 8 eggs)
½ teaspoon cream of tartar

Preheat the oven to 325°F.

Into a medium-size bowl, sift together the flours, baking powder, and salt. Form a well in the center and add the oil, egg yolks, water, vanilla, and maple syrup or honey. Beat with a spoon until smooth. In a large bowl, beat the egg whites with the cream of tartar until very stiff. Pour the batter gradually over the beaten egg whites and gently fold into the egg whites. *Do not stir.* Pour at once into an ungreased 10-inch tube pan. Bake for 65 to 70 minutes, or until the top springs back when lightly touched. Invert on a funnel until the cake has cooled.

Makes 10 to 12 servings.

† **Free of milk, wheat, sugar, corn, citrus**

✦ CHIFFON "POUND" CAKE†

> 1½ cups rice flour
> 6 teaspoons baking powder
> 1 teaspoon salt
> ½ cup oil
> ¾ cup maple syrup or honey
> 6 egg yolks, beaten
> ¼ cup water or coconut milk
> 1 teaspoon vanilla
> 6 egg whites
> ½ teaspoon cream of tartar

Preheat the oven to 350°F.

Mix together the flour, baking powder, and salt. Add the oil, syrup, egg yolks, water, and vanilla. Beat until smooth. Beat the egg whites with cream of tartar until stiff but not dry. Fold into the batter. Pour into an ungreased 13-by-9-inch pan or tube pan. Bake for 35 minutes, until firm to the touch. Invert the pan on a rack to cool.

Makes 10 to 12 servings.

Variations, if Tolerated:
- Add fruit topping if desired.
- Substitute an equal amount of sugar for the honey.
- Substitute an equal amount of milk for the water or coconut milk.

† Free of milk, wheat, sugar, corn, citrus

FROSTINGS

✤§€✤ MAPLE FROSTING*

>   4 teaspoons water
>   1 cup maple sugar

Mix the ingredients together. Let stand for 20 minutes, then spread on cake.

* Suitable for the Elimination Diet

✤§€✤ BLENDER BROILED FROSTING*

>   1 cup honey
>   ½ cup safflower or coconut oil
>   1 teaspoon vanilla
>   2 cups unsweetened shredded coconut

Combine the first three ingredients in a blender. Pour into a mixing bowl and add the coconut. Stir until well mixed. Spread on cake and broil until bubbly, approximately 4 to 5 minutes.

Note: Chopped mixed nuts and/or seeds may be substituted for some or all of the coconut.

* Suitable for the Elimination Diet

❧❀❧ HONEY BUTTER FROSTING†

¼ cup honey
¼ cup butter or allowed margarine
2 cups sifted confectioners' sugar OR 1 to 2 cups tapioca
    flour
1 teaspoon water or milk

Beat the honey and butter together. Add the sugar and water and use to frost cookies.

† **Free of egg, wheat, corn, citrus**

❧❀❧ CONFETTI ICING*

¾ cup unsweetened shredded coconut
Natural food coloring
1½ cups honey
¾ cup water

Color the coconut to a desired shade using natural food coloring. Set aside. Cut the cake up into serving slices or squares. Mix the honey and water together to get a thin, slightly sticky consistency. Drizzle the honey and water mixture over the cake slices and then sprinkle with confetti coconut. The effect is beautiful and the taste is delightfully sweet and moist.

* **Suitable for the Elimination Diet**

PIES

❧❦❧ RICE OR RYE PIE CRUST*

Since this crust is tender, it should be baked in 6 individual tart pans to eliminate cutting and transferring to a serving plate.

> 1 cup rice or rye flour
> ½ teaspoon salt
> ⅓ cup shortening
> 3 tablespoons cold water

Preheat the oven to 450°F.

Mix the flour and salt. Using a pastry blender or fork, cut in the shortening until the size of peas. Sprinkle with water, a tablespoon at a time. Blend lightly with a fork until all the flour is moistened. Form into a ball. Divide the ball of dough into sixths and roll each section between squares of waxed paper until about ⅛ inch thick. Remove the top paper. Turn the pastry into 4-inch tart shells. Remove the remaining paper. Carefully fit the pastry into the tart shell. Flute the edges and prick the pastry several times on the bottom and sides with a fork. Repeat for the remaining balls of dough. Bake for 10 to 12 minutes.

Makes 6 tart shells.

* Suitable for the Elimination Diet

❧ OATMEAL PIE SHELL*

¾ cup oat flour
⅓ cup hot water

Preheat the oven to 325°F.

Mix the flour and hot water together. Press into a 9-inch pie pan. Prick with a fork all over. Bake for 15 minutes (microwave 3 to 4 minutes) or until done.

Makes 1 pie shell.

* **Suitable for the Elimination Diet**

❧ PUMPKIN PECAN PIE*

1 *unbaked* 9-inch oatmeal pie shell (recipe, page 161)
Egg replacer equivalent to 3 eggs
1 cup mashed pumpkin
1 to 1¼ cups maple sugar or maple syrup
1 teaspoon vanilla
1 teaspoon cinnamon (optional)
¼ teaspoon sea salt
1 cup chopped pecans

Preheat the oven to 350°F.

Mix the egg replacer with the remaining ingredients and pour into the pie shell. Bake for about 40 minutes.

Makes 6 servings.

Variations, if Tolerated:
— Substitute an equal amount of sugar for the maple sugar.
— Substitute 3 eggs for the egg replacer.

* **Suitable for the Elimination Diet**

❧❧ PEACH PIE WITH ALMOND CRUST*

> 1 ½ to 2 cups finely ground unblanched almonds
> 1 envelope unflavored gelatin
> ¼ cup hot water
> ¼ cup cold water
> ½ cup honey
> ¼ teaspoon sea salt
> 2 tablespoons pineapple juice
> 1 ½ cups crushed peaches with juice

Line a 9-inch pie pan with the ground almonds. Combine the gelatin and hot water. Let stand for 3 minutes. Add the cold water and stir until the gelatin is dissolved. Add the honey, salt, and juice. Chill. When partially set, beat until light and fluffy. Fold in the peaches with juice. Gently pour into the prepared shell. Chill until firm (2 to 3 hours).

Makes about 8 servings.

Variations, if Tolerated:
– Substitute an equal amount of sugar for the honey.
– Substitute an equal amount of lemon juice for the pineapple juice.

* Suitable for the Elimination Diet

✑✑ STRAWBERRY PIE*

> 1 baked oatmeal pie shell (recipe, page 161)
> 1 envelope unflavored gelatin
> ¼ cup cold water
> ½ cup honey
> ¼ teaspoon sea salt
> 2 tablespoons pineapple juice
> ¾ cup pureed strawberries
> ¾ cup sliced strawberries

Combine the gelatin and water. Soak for 3 minutes. Add the honey, salt, juice, and pureed strawberries. Chill. When partially set, fold in the sliced strawberries. Turn into the pie shell. Chill until firm (2 to 3 hours).

Makes 6 servings.

Variations, if Tolerated:
- Substitute an equal amount of sugar for the honey.
- Substitute 1 tablespoon lemon juice for the pineapple juice.

* Suitable for the Elimination Diet

PUDDINGS

✿✿✿ RICE BROWN BETTY*

8 tart apples, peeled, cored, and sliced
½ cup raisins
½ cup honey
½ cup apple juice or water
¼ cup maple sugar
3 tablespoons rice flour
1 teaspoon cinnamon (optional)
½ cup rolled oats
½ cup rice flour
¼ cup honey
½ cup sunflower seeds
4 tablespoons allowed margarine

Preheat the oven to 350°F. Grease an 11-by-17-inch pan.

Combine the apples, raisins, ½ cup honey, juice, sugar, 3 tablespoons flour, and cinnamon. Turn into the baking pan. Combine the oats, ½ cup rice flour, ¼ cup honey, sunflower seeds, and margarine. Mix well. Spread over the apple mixture. Bake for 45 to 50 minutes.

Makes 9 to 10 servings.

Variations, if Tolerated:
– Substitute an equal amount of sugar for the honey.
– Substitute an equal amount of milk for the apple juice or water.
– Substitute an equal amount of wheat flour for the rice flour.

* Suitable for the Elimination Diet

❧ HASTY PUDDING*

  ¾ cup maple syrup
  ⅓ cup water
  ¾ cup tapioca starch
  1½ teaspoons baking powder
  ½ teaspoon sea salt
  ¼ cup maple sugar
  ½ cup nut, soy, or goat's milk
  1 teaspoon vanilla
  ¼ cup allowed margarine, melted
  ¼ cup raisins or chopped nuts

Preheat the oven to 350°F. Grease a 1-quart casserole.

Bring the syrup and water to a boil in a saucepan. Mix the tapioca starch, baking powder, salt, sugar, nut milk, vanilla, and margarine in a bowl until smooth. Pour into the casserole dish. Sprinkle with raisins or nuts. Pour the boiling syrup over the batter (it makes a sauce in the bottom of the pan after the pudding is baked). Bake for 35 to 40 minutes. Serve with nut or soy milk, if desired.

Makes 3 to 4 servings.

Variations, if Tolerated:
— Serve warm with light cream.
— Substitute an equal amount of milk for the nut, soy, or goat's milk.
— Use 1 cup wheat flour in place of the tapioca starch.

* Suitable for the Elimination Diet

❧❧ RICE PUDDING*

¼ to ½ cup cooked rice
1 cup nut, soy, or goat's milk
¼ cup honey
1 teaspoon vanilla
½ cup raisins

Preheat the oven to 325°F. Grease a 9-by-5-inch loaf pan.

Mix all the ingredients together and pour into the loaf pan. Bake for about 1 hour.

Makes 6 servings.

Variations, if Tolerated:
— Substitute an equal amount of sugar for the honey.
— Substitute an equal amount of milk for the nut or soy milk.

* **Suitable for the Elimination Diet**

❦ FRUITY RICE PUDDING*

1½ teaspoons unflavored gelatin
¼ cup cold water
⅓ cup hot pineapple juice
2 tablespoons maple sugar or honey
⅛ teaspoon sea salt
½ cup cooked rice
½ cup diced canned pineapple and/or peaches
1 teaspoon vanilla

Soak the gelatin in cold water. Dissolve the soaked gelatin in the hot pineapple juice. Add the maple sugar and salt. Chill until slightly thickened. Add the cooked rice, fruit, and vanilla. Turn into a mold and chill until firm.

Note: Other fruit combinations can be used.

Makes 4 servings.

Variations, if Tolerated:
– Substitute an equal amount of sugar for the honey.

* **Suitable for the Elimination Diet**

❧ APPLE TAPIOCA*

¼ cup Minute Tapioca
2½ cups apple juice
Dash of sea salt
⅓ cup honey

Mix together all the ingredients and let stand for 5 minutes. Bring to a boil over a medium heat, stirring often. Cool for 20 minutes. Stir well. Serve warm or cold.

Makes 3 to 4 servings.

Variations, if Tolerated:
– Substitute an equal amount of sugar for the honey.
* **Suitable for the Elimination Diet**

❧ APPLE TAPIOCA SUPREME*

⅓ cup Minute Tapioca
¾ cup honey
4 cups peeled and sliced tart apples
2 cups water
2 tablespoons pineapple or apple juice
2 tablespoons milk-free, corn-free margarine
½ teaspoon sea salt
½ teaspoon cinnamon (optional)

Mix together all the ingredients except the cinnamon in a saucepan and let stand for 5 minutes. Bring to a boil, stirring often. Simmer until the apples are tender (about 12 minutes). Serve with a sprinkle of cinnamon, if desired.

Makes 8 servings.

Variations, if Tolerated:
– Substitute an equal amount of sugar for the honey.
– Substitute 1 tablespoon lemon juice for the pineapple juice.
* **Suitable for the Elimination Diet**

17 · STAPLES, CONDIMENTS, SAUCES, AND SPREADS

During the elimination diet, it can be difficult to find staples that avoid all of the suspected food allergens. In this chapter there are recipes that take the place of such convenience foods as mayonnaise, sour cream, whipped cream, and cottage cheese. There are also recipes for spreads and homemade sauces, including Catsup, Tomato Sauce, White Sauce, and Tartar Sauce.

Look through the appendix on food sources for possible staples that are acceptable on your maintenance diet.

RECIPES

STAPLES AND CONDIMENTS

~§¿~ OAT NOODLES*

These noodles can be dried and then stored in an airtight container. They can also be frozen for later use.

> 1/4 cup water
> 1 cup oat flour
> 1/2 teaspoon salt

Sift the flour and salt together in a large bowl. Form a well in the center of the flour mixture and add the water. Slowly stir the flour into the water until combined. Cover the bowl and let stand for an hour.

On an oat-floured board, roll out the dough 1/16 inch thick. Cut into strips 1 inch thick, then slice each strip crosswise into 1/4- to 1/2-inch-wide noodles. Spread the noodles out on a floured surface and allow to dry for several hours. Cook in plenty of boiling, salted water for 10 to 12 minutes.

Variations, if Tolerated:
- Beat one egg into the water until frothy.
- Substitute other types of flour for the oat flour.

* Suitable for the Elimination Diet

⋑⋐⋐ CATSUP*

½ cup apple cider vinegar
½ teaspoon whole cloves
1 2-inch stick cinnamon
½ teaspoon celery seed
4 pounds tomatoes (about 12 medium tomatoes), washed and quartered
¼ cup water
½ onion, finely chopped
⅛ teaspoon black pepper
¼ cup honey
2 teaspoons salt

Combine the vinegar, cloves, cinnamon, and celery seed in a small covered saucepan. Bring to a boil. Remove from the heat and let stand. In a large kettle or Dutch oven, cook the tomatoes, water, onion, and pepper over medium heat until the tomatoes are quite soft. Put the tomato mixture through a sieve or food mill and return to the heat. Add the honey or allowed sweetener and salt. Bring to a boil. Reduce the heat and simmer until the volume has been reduced by half. Strain the vinegar mixture into the tomato mixture, discarding the spices. Continue simmering until the desired consistency is reached, stirring frequently. Pour into sterilized canning jars, leaving ½ inch of headspace, and seal. Process in a boiling water bath for 5 minutes, or cool and refrigerate in a covered container.

Makes 2 cups.

Variations, if Tolerated:
– Substitute an equal amount of sugar for the honey.

* Suitable for the Elimination Diet

RECIPES

❧ CORN-FREE BAKING POWDER*

¼ cup baking soda
½ cup cream of tartar
¼ cup potato starch

Sift each ingredient before measuring. Mix together thoroughly and sift again. Keep the baking powder dry in a tightly covered jar. To check if the baking powder is still active, add several drops of water to a small amount. If it bubbles vigorously, the baking powder is still good. Use as you would any commercial double-acting baking powder.

Makes ¾ cup.

* **Suitable for the Elimination Diet**

❧ EGGLESS MAYONNAISE*

1½ tablespoons rice flour
½ teaspoon salt
¼ teaspoon dry mustard
¼ cup cold water
¾ cup boiling water
1 tablespoon apple cider vinegar
½ cup safflower oil
⅛ teaspoon paprika
Salt and pepper to taste

Combine the flour, salt, dry mustard, and cold water and stir well. Add the boiling water. Stir constantly over medium heat until the mixture thickens and comes to a boil. Cool until lukewarm. Combine the vinegar and oil and add to the mixture slowly, beating constantly. When well blended, beat in the paprika and salt and pepper. Refrigerate in a covered container.

Makes 1½ to 2 cups.

* **Suitable for the Elimination Diet**

SOY "WHIPPED CREAM"*

½ cup soy or cashew milk
¼ teaspoon vanilla
½ cup safflower oil
1 tablespoon honey
Pinch of sea salt

Put the soy milk and vanilla in a blender and blend at medium speed. With blender running, gradually add the oil until the mixture becomes very thick. If necessary, add a little more oil. Blend in the honey and salt.

Makes 1 cup.

* Suitable for the Elimination Diet

TOFU "SOUR CREAM"†

5 tablespoons powdered goat's milk
1 tablespoon lemon juice
1 cup crumbled tofu

Put the ingredients in a blender and blend until smooth. Use as a substitute for sour cream in molded salads or well-seasoned dips.

Note: If you are unable to find powdered goat's milk, you can use nondairy creamer, but read the label carefully. Some nondairy creamers contain sodium caseinate, a milk protein, corn sweeteners, coconut oil, and possibly other allergy-causing ingredients.

Makes 1⅓ cups.

† Free of milk, egg, wheat, sugar, corn

✎ HOMEMADE COTTAGE CHEESE†

Any type of milk can be used. Goat's milk works well, either fresh or powdered (combine 7 rounded tablespoons powdered milk with 2½ cups water). This is a fun recipe for kids to help with, since most children have never seen how "curds and whey" are made.

> 2½ cups milk
> 1½ teaspoons rennet
> Salt and pepper to taste (optional)

In a saucepan, heat the milk until just tepid. Add the rennet and mix well. Pour the milk into a bowl and leave it in a warm place for 15 minutes, or until the milk has set and curds have formed. Pour the milk mixture into the top of a double boiler and gently heat over hot water to a temperature of 110°F (slightly warmer than lukewarm). Stir constantly until the curds and whey separate. Put a strainer over a bowl and line it with several layers of cheesecloth. Pour in the curds and whey. Tie the corners of the cheesecloth together to form a bag and suspend the bag over the bowl for 12 to 24 hours to drain. The cheese can be drained in 2 to 3 hours by gently squeezing the bag from time to time. Put the drained curds in a bowl, mash it with a fork, and season it to taste. For extra flavor, yogurt, herbs, or spices can be added. Covered and stored in the refrigerator, the cottage cheese will keep for up to 1 week.

Makes 4 ounces.

† **Free of egg, wheat, sugar, corn, citrus**

SAUCES

❧ QUICK TOMATO SAUCE*

    ½ cup minced onion
    1 tablespoon allowed oil, such as olive oil
    1 garlic clove, minced (optional)
    6 ounces tomato paste
    1½ cups water
    1 tablespoon minced fresh basil
    1 teaspoon honey

In a medium-size saucepan, sauté the onions in the oil until soft. Add the garlic and sauté for an additional minute. Add the remaining ingredients and simmer for 5 minutes more.

Makes 2 cups.

Variations, if Tolerated:
— Substitute an equal amount of sugar for the honey.

* Suitable for the Elimination Diet

❧ TARTAR SAUCE*

    1 cup homemade mayonnaise (recipe, p. 172)
    1 teaspoon grated onion
    2 tablespoons capers, slightly mashed, OR chopped
        sweet pickles
    1 teaspoon dried parsley, minced
    ¼ teaspoon dry mustard

Mix all ingredients thoroughly and chill. Serve over fish.

Makes 1 cup.

* Suitable for the Elimination Diet

RECIPES

❧❦❧ WHITE SAUCE*

  1 tablespoon milk-free, corn-free margarine
  1½ teaspoons potato starch or acceptable flour
  ¼ teaspoon salt
  ½ cup soy milk
  1 teaspoon dried parsley (optional)

Melt the margarine in a saucepan over medium heat. Add the potato starch and salt and stir until mixed well. Add the soy milk and parsley. Continue to stir until the mixture thickens.

Makes ¾ cups.

Variations, if Tolerated:
– In place of potato starch, try Cream of Rice, Minute Tapioca, wheat, rice flour, or barley and increase or decrease the amount to thicken the sauce.

* Suitable for the Elimination Diet

SPREADS

❧❦❧ MAPLE BUTTER SPREAD*

  1 cup maple syrup
  ¾ cup melted milk-free, corn-free margarine

Cook the maple syrup over medium heat until a small amount forms a soft ball in cold water. Add the margarine and beat until thick and creamy. Serve warm on waffles or hot biscuits and cold on slices of bread.

Makes 1½ cups.

* Suitable for the Elimination Diet

❧§❧ APPLE HONEY BUTTER*

3½ pounds apples, peeled, cored, and chopped
1 to 1½ cups honey
½ cup apple vinegar
½ cup crushed pineapple

Preheat the oven to 300°F.

In a medium-size saucepan over low heat, cook the apples until soft. (No water is necessary, since there is enough moisture in the apples.) Press through a food mill to make 8 cups of applesauce. Combine the applesauce with honey, vinegar, and pineapple in a large 6-quart pan. Bake for 3 hours, stirring occasionally. Pour hot into hot clean pint jars, leaving ¼ inch of headspace. Adjust the caps. Process for 10 minutes in a water bath at simmering temperature (180 to 185°F). When cool, check the seals.

Makes 6 cups.

* Suitable for the Elimination Diet

❧§❧ NUT BUTTER*

1½ cups chopped nuts, such as peanuts, almonds, or
   cashews
1 to 3 tablespoons safflower oil
¼ teaspoon sea salt

Preheat the oven to 350°F.

Spread the nuts in a shallow pan. Sprinkle with oil and salt. Bake for 10 to 15 minutes or until toasted. Place the nuts in a blender. Process at medium speed until smooth and creamy. Pour into a covered container and store in the refrigerator or freezer. Stir to blend in the oil before using.

Makes 1 cup.

* Suitable for the Elimination Diet

❧ STRAWBERRY JAM†

2 tablespoons lemon juice
1 envelope unflavored gelatin
2 tablespoons water
1½ teaspoons arrowroot
2 cups fresh strawberries
4 to 4½ tablespoons honey or maple syrup

Combine the lemon juice, gelatin, water, and arrowroot. Heat in a saucepan, stirring constantly. Lower the heat, add the berries and sweetener, and heat to boiling. Boil for 3 minutes. Pour into jars and refrigerate or freeze.

Makes 2 cups.

Variations, if Tolerated:
— Substitute an equal amount of cornstarch for the arrowroot.

† **Free of milk, egg, wheat, corn**

❧ BLUEBERRY JAM†

4 cups fresh blueberries
2 cups sugar
1 envelope unflavored gelatin
1 teaspoon lemon extract

In a large saucepan, slightly crush half the berries. Add the remaining berries, sugar, and gelatin. Heat to boiling, stirring constantly. Boil hard for 2 minutes, stirring constantly. Stir in the lemon extract. Pour into clean jelly glasses or jars. Seal the jars or freeze.

Makes 3 half-pints.

† **Free of milk, egg, wheat, corn**

APPENDIXES

FOOD SOURCES

The food companies listed below produce foods that are free of some of the most common allergens. Be sure to check the labels since the ingredients may have changed. Look for different types of foods in your area.

AFTER THE FALL PRODUCTS, INC.
P.O. Box 777
Brattleboro, VT 05301

Apple Juice
Apple/Raspberry Juice
Apple/Apricot Juice
Apple/Pineapple Juice
Apple/Cherry Juice
Apple/Grape Juice
Apple/Blackberry Juice
Pure Pear Juice

AMERICAN MAPLE PRODUCTS CORP.
Newport, VT 05855

Old Colony Pure Maple Sugar Candy (100% pure)
Old Colony Pure Maple Butter Spread (100% pure; whipped)
Old Colony Pure Maple Syrup (100% pure)
Old Colony Granulated Maple Sugar (100% pure; comes in shaker dispenser or hard slabs)

ARROWHEAD MILLS, INC.
110 South Lawton
Hereford, TX 79045

Arrowhead Mills oils (no preservatives, unrefined; corn, olive, safflower, sesame)
Deaf Smith Peanut Butter (100% peanuts)
Arrowhead Mills organic grains, seeds, and nuts
Arrowhead Mills Sesame Tahini (100% organically grown sesame seeds)

CASTLE & COOKE FOODS
P.O. Box 3928
San Francisco, CA 94119

Dole Pineapple in its own juice
Dole Pineapple Juice, unsweetened
Bumble Bee tuna, salmon, and oysters (water pack; read tuna labels carefully; some contain vegetable broth)

CHICO-SAN, INC.
1062 Progress St.
Pittsburgh, PA 15212

Rice Cakes (whole brown rice, sesame seeds, and salt)
Yinnie's Taffy (rice, water, barley malt)
Yinnie's Rice Syrup (rice, water, barley malt)
Yinnie's Caramel (oat powder, raisins, almonds, sesame oil, coconut, lecithin [from sesame seeds], natural vanilla, agar)
Miso (soybeans)
Seaweeds

CZIMER FOOD, INC.
P.O. Box 285
Lockport, IL 60441

Organic foods, exotic meats, and fish
Mail orders accepted.

DUFFY MOTTS CO., INC.
New York, NY 10017

Mott's Natural Style Applesauce (100% apples)
Mott's Natural Style Apple Juice (100% apple juice)

EDEN FOODS
701 Clinton-Tecumseh Hwy.
Clinton, MI 49236

100% buckwheat noodles

EL MOLINO MILLS
Div., American Health Products Co.
33 Kings Highway
Orangeburg, NY 10962

Sunflower and sesame seeds (no preservatives or additives)
Cara Coa Carob Powder (100% carob)
Brown rice (natural, unpolished, 100% pure)
Rolled oats, puffed rice cereal (100% whole grain, no sugar or
   additives)

ELAM'S
2625 Gardner Road
Broadview, IL 60153

Elam's Brown Rice Flour
Elam's Scotch Style Oatmeal (stoneground)
Elam's Steel Cut Oatmeal
Elam's Soy Flour
Mail orders accepted.

FOOD SOURCES

ENER-G FOODS, INC.
P.O. Box 24723
Seattle, WA 98124–0723

Aglutella Spaghetti
Aglutella Macaroni (cornstarch, rice starch, potato starch, monoglycerides, carotene)
Arrowroot Starch
Unsweetened Coconut
Ener-G Barley Mix
Ener-G Rice Mix
Ener-G Oat Mix
Ener-G Brown Rice Flour
Ener-G Potato Starch
Ener-G Potato Flour
Ener-G Xanthan Gum
Ener-G Mayonnaise
Ener-G Egg Replacer
Soyquick
Nutquik
Plus many low-allergen foods

FEARN NATURAL FOODS
Div. of Modern Products, Inc.
P.O. Box 09398
Milwaukee, WI 53209

Fearn brown rice baking mix
Fearn rice baking mix
Fearn rice flour
Fearn natural soya powder
Fearn breakfast patty mix
Fearn sunflower burger mix

GENERAL FOODS CORP.
White Plains, NY 10625

Bird's Eye Sweet Green Peas (frozen, 100% green peas)
Bird's Eye Chopped Broccoli (frozen, 100% broccoli)
Minute Tapioca
"Plain" Bird's Eye Frozen Vegetables (except corn)

HAIN PURE FOOD CO., INC.
13660 S. Figueroa
Los Angeles, CA 90061

Hain Natural Potato Chips (safflower oil)
Hain Eggless Mayonnaise (soy, water, honey, cider, vinegar, lemon juice, natural spices, algin, onion oil)
Hain Safflower Margarine (safflower, soybean, water, salt, lecithin, colored with carotene)
Hain Soy Oil Shortening (solid soy, vitamin E)
Hain nut butters: almond, cashew, peanut, sesame
Hain preserves: apple, apricot, grape, orange marmalade, red raspberry, seedless blackberry, strawberry
Hain Cider Vinegar
Hain Sea Salt
Hain Natural Imitation Catsup

HEALTH VALLEY NATURAL FOODS, INC.
700 Union St.
Montebello, CA 90640

Potato Chips (potato, safflower oil, sunflower oil, salt; no additives)
Catch-Up (tomatoes, water, honey, sea salt, natural seasonings)
Tamari-Ya Soy Sauce (water, soybeans, sea salt)
Soy-Moo (water, dehulled soybeans, honey)
Plus other products

HERSHEY IMPORT CO., INC.
700 E. Lincoln Ave.
Rahway, NJ 07065

Love Snacks Pineapple Snacks (pineapple and honey; no additives)
Love Snacks Fruity Mix (dates, almonds, cashews, dry-roasted peanuts, walnuts, pineapple, unsweetened coconut, filberts, apricots)
Love Snacks Monukka Nut Mix (raisins, peanuts, coconut oil, sea salt)
Plus seeds, grains, beans, and nuts

HOLLYWOOD HEALTH FOODS
Los Angeles, CA 90061
Pure Safflower Oil

HUNT'S WESSON FOODS, INC.
Fullerton, CA 92634
Hunt's Tomato Paste

JACKSON-MITCHELL, INC.
1240 South Street
P.O. Box 934
Turlock, CA 95381

Meyenberg Whole Fresh Goat's Milk, canned and evaporated
goat's milk

LA PREFERIDA, INC.
3400 W. 35th St.
Chicago, IL 60632

Dry red kidney beans, chick-peas, and pinto beans

MIDWEST NUT AND SEED CO., INC.
1332 W. Grand
Chicago, IL 60622

Nuts, seeds, beans

THE QUAKER OATS CO.
Industrial Cereals Dept.
Merchandise Mart Plaza
Chicago, IL 60654

Old Fashioned Quaker Oats (100% oats)
Quick Quaker Oats (100% oats)
Quick-Cooking Barley
Arden Rice Cakes

REJUZENATIVE FOODS
P.O. Box 8464
Santa Cruz, CA 95061

Fermented raw vegetables

SANDOZ NUTRITION
5320 W. 23rd St.
P.O. Box 370
Minneapolis, MN 55440

Featherweight Cereal-Free Baking Powder
Featherweight water-packed fruits and vegetables; all 100% pure.
Mail orders accepted.

SHEDD'S FOOD PRODUCTS
Detroit, MI 48238

Willow Run margarine

J. M. SMUCKER CO.
Orville, OH 44667

Natural peanut butter (peanuts, salt)

SUN-MAID GROWERS OF CALIFORNIA
Kingburg, CA 93631

Sun-Maid Sun Dried Seedless Raisins (100% sun dried without
   preservatives)
Note: Other Sun-Maid products may have sulphur dioxide added,
so use *only* sun dried dark raisins.

THREE DIAMOND
Distributed by Mitsutushi International Corp.
Chicago, IL 60611

Pineapple in its own juice
Light tuna in water
Whole oysters with salt and water
Water chestnuts in water

TILLIE LEWIS FOOD
Division of Ogden Food Products
Stockton, CA 95201

Tasti Diet fruits and vegetables (canned)

VERMONT COUNTRY MAPLE, INC.
P.O. Box 53
Jerico Center, VT 05465

Pure maple syrup
Pure maple sugar granules

WELCH FOODS, INC.
Westfield, NY 14787

Welch's Grape Juice (from concentrate; vitamin C, no artificial flavors or colors)

WESTBRAE NATURAL FOODS
P.O. Box 8711
4240 Hollis St.
Emeryville, CA 94662

Stoneground Mustard (mustard seeds, vinegar distilled from grain, salt, natural spices and herbs; no artificial colors, flavors, or sugar)
Specialty butters
Plus many other items

BIOLOGICAL CLASSIFICATIONS OF FOODS

The following lists contain detailed information on the relationships of many common foods. Familiarizing yourself with these charts will enable you to check on food families to which you may be sensitive. For example, if you are allergic to tomatoes, you may also be sensitive to eggplant or potatoes, which are all in the Potato (Nightshade) Family. Or if grains are a problem, you can substitute items from different families, such as tapioca starch or potato starch.

By being aware of these food families, you can avoid items to which you may be cross-sensitive and find appropriate substitutes.

APPLE FAMILY
Apple
  Cider
  Juice
  Vinegar
  Apple pectin
Pear
Quince
  Quince seed

ARROWROOT FAMILY
Arrowroot

ARUM FAMILY
Dasheen
Malanga
Taro
  Poi
Yautia

BANANA FAMILY
Banana
Plantain

BEECH FAMILY
Beechnut
Chestnut

BIRCH FAMILY
Filbert
Hazelnut
Oil of birch (wintergreen)

BORAGE FAMILY
Borage
Comfrey

BRAZILNUT FAMILY
Brazil nut

BUCKWHEAT FAMILY
Buckwheat
Rhubarb
Sorrel

CACTUS FAMILY
Prickly pear
Tequila

CALTRAP FAMILY
Gum guaiac

CAPER FAMILY
Capers

CASHEW FAMILY
Cashew
Mango
Pistachio

CHINESE WATER CHESTNUT FAMILY
Chestnuts, Chinese

CITRUS FAMILY
Citron
Grapefruit
Kumquat
Lemon
Lime
Orange
Tangerine

COMPOSITE FAMILY
Absinthe
Artichoke, Common
Celtuce
Chamomile
Chicory
Dandelion
Endive
Escarole
Goldenrod
Lettuce
    Head
    Leaf
Jerusalem artichoke
Oyster plant
    Salsify
Ragweed and Pyrethrum
    and other related inhalants
Romaine lettuce
Safflower
Sesame seed
Sunflower
Sagebrush
    Wormwood
Tarragon

EBONY FAMILY
Persimmon

FUNGI FAMILY
Mushroom
Yeast

GINGER FAMILY
Cardamom
Ginger
Turmeric

GINSENG FAMILY
Ginseng

GOOSEBERRY FAMILY
Currant
Gooseberry

GOOSEFOOT FAMILY
Beet
  Beet sugar
Chard
  Swiss chard
Lamb's quarters
Spinach
Thistle

GOURD FAMILY
Cantaloupe
Casaba
Christmas melon
Cucumber
Gherkin
Honeydew
Muskmelon
Persian melon
Pumpkin
Squash
  Summer
  Winter
Watermelon
Zucchini

GRAINS (CEREAL, GRASSES) FAMILY
Barley
  Malt
  Maltose
Bamboo shoots
Cane
  Cane sugar
    Turbinado
  Molasses
  Rum
Corn
  Cornmeal
  Cornstarch
  Corn oil
  Corn sugar
    "Cerelose"
    Dextrose
    "Dyno"
  Corn syrup
    Cartose
    Glucose
    "Sweetose"
    Grits
    Hominy
    Whiskey/bourbon
Millet
Oats
Popcorn
Rice
Rye
Sorghum
  Kafir
  Molasses
Triticale
Wheat
  Bran
  "Farina"

Flour
  Graham
  Gluten
  Patent
  Semolina flour
Wheat germ
  Wild rice

GRAPE FAMILY
Grape
  Brandy (grape)
  Champagne
  Cream of tartar
  Raisin
Grape wine
  Vinegar

HEATH FAMILY
Blueberry
Cranberry
Huckleberry
Wintergreen

HOLLY FAMILY
Bearberry
Maté (or yerba maté)
Pokeberry
Yaupon tea

HONEYSUCKLE FAMILY
Elderberry

IRIS FAMILY
Saffron

KELP FAMILY
Algin

LAUREL FAMILY
Avocado
Bay leaf
Cinnamon
Sassafras

LEGUMES
Alfalfa
Black-eyed pea
Bush bean
Carob
Chick-pea (garbanzo)
Green bean
Green pea
Jack bean
Kidney bean
Lentil
Licorice
Lima bean
Mung bean
Navy bean
Pea
Peanut
  Peanut oil
Pinto bean
Senna
Soybean
  Flour
  Oil
  Lecithin
String bean
Tonka bean
Tragacanth gum

LILY FAMILY
Aloe
Asparagus
Bermuda onion
Chive
Garlic
Leek
Onion
Sarsaparilla
Scallion
Yucca

MACADAMIA FAMILY
Macadamia nut

MADDER FAMILY
Coffee

MALLOW FAMILY
Cottonseed
  Meal
  Oil
Okra (gumbo)

MAPLE FAMILY
Maple sugar
Maple syrup

MAY APPLE FAMILY
May apple

MINT FAMILY
Artichoke, Chinese
Basil
Horehound
Lavender
Marjoram
Mint
Oregano
Peppermint
Rosemary
Sage
Savory
Spearmint
Thyme

MORNING GLORY FAMILY
Sweet potato

MULBERRY FAMILY
Breadfruit
Fig
Hops
Mulberry

MUSTARD FAMILY
Broccoli
Brussels sprout
Cabbage
Cauliflower
Celery cabbage
Collard
Colza shoot
Horseradish
Kale
Kohlrabi
Mustard
Radish
Rutabaga
Turnip
Watercress

MYRTLE FAMILY
Allspice
Cloves
Guava
Paprika
Pimento

BIOLOGICAL CLASSIFICATIONS OF FOODS

NUTMEG FAMILY
Mace
Nutmeg

OAK FAMILY
Chestnut

OLIVE FAMILY
Black olive (ripe)
  Olive oil
Green olive

ORCHID FAMILY
Vanilla

PALM FAMILY
Coconut
  Oil
Date
Palm cabbage
Sago

PAPAL FAMILY
Papaya
  Papain

PARSLEY FAMILY
Angelica
Anise
Caraway
Carrot
Celeriac
Celery
Celery seed
Chervil
Coriander
Cumin
Dill
Fennel
Lovage
Parsley
Parsnip
Water celery

PAWPAW FAMILY
Pawpaw

PEPPER FAMILY
Black pepper
White pepper

PINE FAMILY
Juniper
Piñon nut (pignolia)
  Pine nut

PINEAPPLE FAMILY
Pineapple

PLUM FAMILY
Almond
Apricot
Cherry
  Sour
  Sweet
  Wild
Nectarine
Peach
Plum
  Prune

POMEGRANATE FAMILY
Pomegranate

POPPY FAMILY
Poppy seed

POTATO (NIGHTSHADE) FAMILY
Belladonna
Eggplant
Ground cherry
Peppers
  Chili
    Cayenne
    Red
  Green
  Red sweet
  Paprika
Potato
Tobacco
Tomato

PURSLANE FAMILY
New Zealand spinach
Purslane

ROSE FAMILY
Blackberry
Boysenberry
Dewberry
Loganberry
Raspberry
  Black
  Red
Strawberry
Youngberry

SAPODILLA FAMILY
Chicle

SOAPBERRY FAMILY
Litchi nut

SPURGE FAMILY
Cassava (Yuca)
  Tapioca

STERCULIA FAMILY
Cacao
  Chocolate
  Cocoa
Cola
  Caffeine
Karaya gum
Kola bean

TEA FAMILY
Tea
  Black
  Green

WALNUT FAMILY
Butternut
Hickory
Pecan
Walnut
  Black
  English

YAM FAMILY
Chinese potato
Yam

MISCELLANEOUS
Honey

ANIMAL CLASSIFICATIONS

AMPHIBIAN
Frog

BIRDS
Chicken
  Chicken eggs
Duck
  Duck eggs
Goose
  Goose eggs
Grouse
Guinea hen
Partridge
Peacock
Pheasant
Pigeon
Quail
Squab
Turkey
  Turkey eggs

CRUSTACEANS
Decapods
  Crab
  Crayfish
  Lobster
  Prawn
  Shrimp

MAMMALS
Antelope
Bear
Beaver
Bovine
  Beef (cattle)
    Gelatin (beef)
    Cow's milk
      Butter
      Cheese
      Lactose (milk sugar)
    Veal
Bison
Buffalo
Goat
  Milk
  Cheese
Sheep
  Lamb
  Mutton
Deer
  Caribou
  Deer (venison)
  Elk
  Moose
  Reindeer
Dolphin
Pig (pork)
  Bacon
  Ham
  Lard
Rabbit
  Cottontail
  Hare
  Jackrabbit
Squirrel
Whale

MOLLUSKS
Cephalopods
  Octopus
  Squid
Gastropods
  Abalone
  Snail
Pelecypods
  Clam
  Cockle
  Mussel
  Oyster
  Quahog
  Scallop

REPTILES
Alligator
Rattlesnake
Turtle

FISHES (SALTWATER)
Anchovy Family
  Anchovy
Barracuda Family
  Barracuda
Bluefish Family
  Bluefish
Codfish Family
  Cod (scrod)
  Cusk
  Haddock
  Hake
  Pollack
Croaker Family
  Croaker
  Drum
  Sea trout
  Silver perch
  Spot
  Weakfish (spotted sea trout)

Dolphin Family
  Dolphin
  Mahi mahi
Eel Family
  American eel
Flounder Family
  Dab
  Flounder
  Halibut
  Plaice
  Sole
  Turbot
Harvestfish Family
  Butterfish
  Harvestfish
Herring Family
  Menhaden
  Pilchard (sardine)
  Sea herring
  Shad
Jack Family
  Aberjack
  Pompano
  Yellow jack
Mackerel Family
  Albacore
  Bonito
  Mackerel
  Skipjack
  Tuna
Marlin Family
  Marlin
  Sailfish
Mullet Family
  Mullet
Porgy Family
  Northern scup (porgy)

Sea Bass Family
   Grouper
   Sea bass
   Red snapper
Scorpionfish Family
   Rosefish (ocean perch)
Sea Catfish Family
   Ocean catfish
Shark Family
   Shark
   Monk
Silverside Family
   Silverside (whitebait)
Swordfish Family
   Swordfish
Tarpon Family
   Tarpon
Tilefish Family
   Tilefish

FISHES (FRESHWATER)

Bass Family
   White perch
   Yellow bass
Catfish Family
   Bullhead
   Catfish species
Croaker Family
   Fresh water drum
Herring Family
   Shad (roe)

Minnow Family
   Carp
   Chub
Paddlefish Family
   Paddlefish
Perch Family
   Sauger
   Walleye, Pike
   Yellow perch
Pike Family
   Pickerel
   Pike, Northern
   Muskellunge
Salmon Family
   Salmon species
   Trout species
Smelt Family
   Smelt
Sturgeon Family
   Sturgeon (caviar)
Sucker Family
   Buffalofish
   Sucker
Sunfish Family
   Black bass species
   Sunfish species
   Crappie
Whitefish Family
   Whitefish

RECIPES FOR THE
ELIMINATION DIET

CHAPTER 12   SOUPS AND STEWS

Bean Soup
Beef and Vegetable Stew
Beef Stock
Chicken and Potato Soup
Chicken Soup
Chicken Stock
Irish Lamb Stew
Minestrone
Pea Soup
Tomato Soup
Vegetable Beef Soup

CHAPTER 13   VEGETABLES AND SIDE DISHES

Baked Sweet Potato Casserole
Barley and Mushroom Pilaf
Braised Celery
China Bowl Rice Sticks
Confetti Rice
Cranberry Relish
Dilled Carrots
Eggplant with Tomato
Green Beans with Almonds
Hash Brown Potatoes
Maple Carrots
Oriental Tomato Skillet
Rice Pilaf
Stuffed Mushrooms

CHAPTER 14   MAIN COURSES

Baked Chicken with Tomato
    Rice Stuffing
Broiled Burgers
Chicken Chop Suey
Chicken or Turkey Loaf
Chicken Supreme
Honey Baked Chicken
Lamb Pilaf
Pineapple Pork Chops with
    Rice
Pork Chop Spanish Rice
Quick Savory Meat Loaf
Sloppy Joes

CHAPTER 15   COOKIES, BARS, FRUIT TREATS, AND SNACKS

Almond Cookies
Almond Crescents
Apple Crisp
Apple Rice Betty
Apple Snack
Applesauce
Applesauce Cookies
Baked Pears
Banana Oatmeal Cookies
Blueberry Delight Cookies
Butterscotch Cookies
Cantaloupe Sherbet
Carob Candy
Coconut-Covered Raisins
French-Fried Bananas
Frosty Freezer Treats
Fruit Sherbet

RECOMMENDED
READING

BOOKS

Austry, Gloria, and T. D. Allen. *The Color-Coded Allergy Cookbook*. New York: Bobbs-Merrill Co., 1983.

Breneman, James. *Basics of Food Allergies*. Springfield, IL: Charles C. Thomas, 1978.

————, ed. *Handbook of Food Allergy*. New York: Marcel-Dekker, 1986.

Crook, William. *The Yeast Connection*. Jackson, TN: Professional Books, 1985.

Dong, Faye. *All About Food Allergy*. Philadelphia: George Stickley Co., 1984.

Frazier, Claude. *Coping with Food Allergies: Symptoms and Treatment*. New York: Quadrangle/The New York Times Book Co., 1974.

Gerrard, John W. *Food Allergy: New Perspectives*. Springfield, IL: Charles C. Thomas, 1980.

Gonshorowski, Addie. *The Sugarless Cookbook*. Eugene, OR: Ad-Dee Publishers, 1981.

Hamrick, Becky, and S. L. Wiesenfeld. *The Egg-Free, Milk-Free, Wheat-Free Cookbook*. New York: Harper & Row Publishers, 1982.

Hills, Hilary C. *Good Food, Gluten-Free*. New Canaan, CT: Keats Publishing Co., 1976.

RECOMMENDED READING

————. *Good Food, Milk-Free, Grain-Free.* New Canaan, CT: Keats Publishing Co., 1980.

Hostage, Jacqueline. *Living . . . Without Milk.* New York: Betterway Publications, 1979.

Jones, Marge. *The Allergy Cookbook.* Emmaus, PA: Rodale Press, 1984.

Nonken, Pamela P., and S. Roger Hirsch. *The Allergy Cookbook and Food Buying Guide.* New York: Warner Books, 1982.

Rudoff, Carol. *The Allergy Baker.* Menlo Park, CA: Prologue Publications, 1981.

Speer, Frederick. *Food Allergy.* Littleton, MA: PSG Publishing Co., 1979.

Stevens, Laura. *The Complete Book of Allergy Control.* New York: Macmillan Publishing Co., 1983.

Thomas, Linda. *Caring and Cooking for the Allergic Child.* New York: Sterling Publishing Co., 1980.

Wood, Marion. *Delicious and Easy Rice Flour Recipes.* Springfield, IL: Charles C. Thomas, 1972.

————. *Gourmet Food on a Wheat-Free Diet.* Springfield, IL: Charles C. Thomas, 1967.

OTHER PUBLICATIONS

Bowman, F. *Wheat-, Gluten-, Egg- and Milk-Free Recipes for Use at High Altitudes and at Sea Level.* Colorado State University Experiment Station, Fort Collins, CO 80523 (Bulletin 5445).

Jones, Marge. *Baking with Amaranth.* Illinois Amaranth Co., P.O. Box 464, Mundelein, IL 60060.

Hartsook, Elaine. *Gluten Intolerance Group Cookbook.* Gluten Intolerance Group, 26604 Dover Court, Kent, WA 98031.

Rockwell, Sally. *Coping with Candida.* Diet Design, P.O. Box 15181, Seattle, WA.

Truss, C. O. *The Missing Diagnosis.* Missing Diagnosis, P.O. Box 26508, Birmingham, AL 35226.

INDEX

INDEX

INDEX